Soldiers of the Peninsular War

1808-1814

RENÉ NORTH

ALMARK PUBLISHING CO, LTD, LONDON

First published — April 1972

ISBN 0 85524 066 0 (hard cover edition)
ISBN 0 85524 067 9 (paper covered edition)

By the same Author:
Regiments at Waterloo

Printed in Great Britain by
Martins Press Ltd., London EC1
for the publishers, Almark Publishing Co. Ltd.,
270 Burlington Road, New Malden,
Surrey KT3 4NL, England.

Introduction

THIS book is a companion volume to the same author's earlier work, *Regiments at Waterloo,* and follows generally the same style and format. It provides a comprehensive but concise coverage of the different regiments and units on the British and French sides involved in the long drawn-out Peninsular War of 1808 to 1814, the campaign immediately preceding the decisive '100 Days' which culminated in the Battle of Waterloo and Napoleon's final defeat. Thus the two books between them provide the military uniform and model soldier enthusiast with a handy guide to the soldiers involved in the greater part of the Napoleonic Wars insofar as the Anglo-Allied and French forces are concerned.

The actual course of the Peninsular campaign and its military and political ramifications are outside the scope of this book; several military history books cover the battles and events in exhaustive detail, but there is a chronology of events and a list of some suggested books for further reading in the appendices. This book shows 60 figures in colour, representative of the uniforms worn by both sides in the campaign, and a further 60 figures are shown in line drawings with colour details given in almost every case. By cross-reference between the line drawings and the colour drawings it is in most cases possible to see all round detail on the uniforms featured. Major battles and events concerning the regiments concerned are included in the text. To make best use of available space, particularly in Part 2 some regiments are shown in either colour drawings or line drawings, but not both. In the latter case, colour details are given in either the caption or the text. References to Fig. numbers in the text, eg, 'Fig 10', refer to the relevant colour drawings, all of which are numbered.

This book is the last work of its much-respected author, René North who, sadly, died in 1971 shortly after the bulk of the text and colour art was completed. For assistance in finishing the book with extra illustrations, notes, and appendices, the publishers wish to thank A. H. Bowling, Roy Dilley, and D. S. V. Fosten.

CONTENTS

Section **Page**

Light infantry were an innovation in the British Army arising from experience in the Peninsular War. Sir John Moore adapted the idea from French tactics and organisation. This spirited Simkin print shows the 85th Foot in action at Nivelle, November 1813. The facings (collar and cuffs) are yellow. The drummer shown wears white lace on his red tunic. Note the customary leather reinforcement to the bottoms of the officer's overalls (A. H. Bowling collection).

FRONT COVER: One of the most famous British infantry regiments of the Peninsular War was the 57th Foot which gave distinguished service against great odds at the Battle of Albuhera on May 16, 1811. The regiment suffered 430 casualties (dead and wounded) out of a total strength of 570. The colonel's call to 'Die hard, my men' led to the regiment's subsequent nickname of 'The Diehards'. This print shows the regiment marching past their colonel in Spain before Albuhera; a mounted staff officer with bicorne hat is on the extreme right (A. H. Bowling collection).

Part 1: The British and their Allies

THE Peninsular War was, prior to the Great War, one of the longest and most costly campaigns involving British troops. The war started in 1808, a further phase in the long war against Napoleon's First Empire, and continued until 1814. British forces were involved in more than 20 major battles during this time, plus many lesser actions. 'Albuhera', 'Badajos', 'Salamanca', 'Nivelle', 'Vittoria', 'Corunna' and 'Nive' are among the many battle honours which British regiments were awarded as a result of the campaign.

Life for the British troops in the Peninsula was hard. Supplies were short and there was much 'living off the country', both by scrounging and, on occasion, looting. The weather was often bad and there was mountainous country to be traversed in appalling winter conditions. Sickness was rife and medical attention was rudimentary. British troops acquitted themselves well as did their allies the Portuguese and the men of the King's German Legion. Two arms which made notable contributions to the campaigns of the time were the light dragoons and the Royal Horse Artillery whose dashing mobility had a valuable influence in several critical battles. In this part of the book, though, we deal with the regiments in greater detail in order of seniority.

HOUSEHOLD CAVALRY

Whereas the French army in the field was commanded by the sovereign in person, in Great Britain the position was different. The King stayed at home and delegated his authority to a professional soldier in the person of a Commander-in-Chief. Great Britain's ruler was an amateur soldier, but an hereditary monarch. France's ruler was a professional soldier but an amateur monarch.

Nevertheless, the King's Guards, both Horse and Foot, were treated as normal fighting units and were sent on campaign exactly like troops of the Line, only a few remaining for guard duties in London.

Compared with the French, the number of British Guard regiments was small: three of cavalry, three of infantry, and no artillery at all. The three cavalry regiments were the 1st and 2nd Life Guards and the Royal Horse Guards, all of whom fought in the Peninsular War.

It was never quite clear what difference of uniform existed between the two regiments of Life Guards at this period. Some authorities show different colours of collar-patches, some of shoulder-straps and others of flask-cords; but so far no precise regulations have come to light.

When the Life Guards landed in the Peninsula in 1812, the helmet had recently replaced the rather inconvenient bicorne hat hitherto in wear. However, the rugged nature of the country was unsuitable for operations of heavy

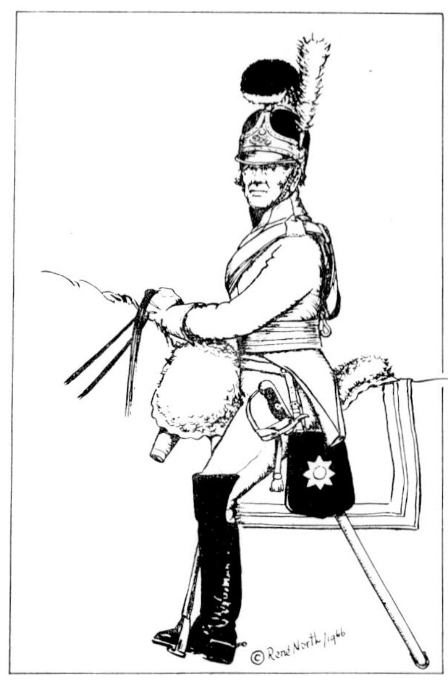

THE LIFE GUARDS

LEFT: Officer in 1813 wearing the bicorne hat which was discarded about this time in favour of the helmet. The coat was red with blue facings and gold lace. RIGHT: Trooper c.1814 in the new crested helmet which was leather with brass bindings. Crest was black and crimson and the plume white. Coatee red. Overalls white.

cavalry—which was probably just as well, for the Life Guards, quite unprepared for active service after a long period of ceremonial in England, had unwisely jettisoned much of their necessaries on the journey. Curry-combs, they surmised, would surely be unnecessary in war.

With the Royal Horse Guards the position was different. Although not officially designated as Household troops until 1820, they were normally brigaded with the Life Guards. They were descended from a regiment of Horse in the Parliamentarian army which was to have been disbanded at the Restoration of 1660. However, on January 26, of the following year, King Charles II ordered its retention, at a strength of 8 troops, under the Earl of Oxford as colonel. Whether this was the origin of the Regiment's uniform of Oxford blue is not quite clear, but at all events that colour, with scarlet facings, has been regulation for the Horse Guards ever since. (Fig 1).

A painting by Denis Dighton in the Royal collection at Windsor shows two officers and some other ranks in a mountainous landscape. They wear high-slung sabretaches bearing a silver star of the Garter surmounted by a crown and surrounded by a wide gold border. The overalls have two gold bands down each side and the shabraque is scarlet, with a gold border and fringe, and the same device as the sabretache in the corners and on the holster-caps.

Other ranks are similarly dressed, except that yellow replaces gold, and the white pouch-belt carries a crimson flask-cord.

The 5th Dragoon Guards in action at the Battle of Vittoria on June 21, 1813. They are wearing the helmet which had been introduced in place of the bicorne the previous year. For basic uniform colours see Fig 4, page 20. Facings are green. French line infantry men can also be seen (A. H. Bowling collection).

DRAGOON GUARDS

These troops formed the seven regiments of heavy cavalry in the British army, and of these the 3rd, 4th and 5th were employed in the Peninsula; rather surprisingly, in a sense, because the apparent absence of their French counterparts (the Cuirassiers) in the campaign would suggest that the mountainous state of the country was unsuitable for heavy cavalry.

All three regiments were raised in 1685 and in the early 19th Century were dressed alike (Figs 2-4). They were distinguished by facing colours worn on collar and cuffs, as follows: 3rd white; 4th, blue and 5th, green; while the lace—gold or silver for officers—was yellow for the 3rd and 5th, and white for the 4th. In addition, the title of the regiment appeared in a small oval device at the base of the helmet-plate.

The 3rd Dragoon Guards were originally cuirassiers and after Sedgemoor its six troops became the 4th Regiment of Horse. It landed at Lisbon on April 26-27, 1809, and was first in action at Talavera and afterwards at Albuhera. At Usagre the Regiment encountered the 4th, 20th and 26th French Dragoons on its flank, but assisted by the 4th Dragoons, it charged and overthrew the enemy. Many of the French, taken by surprise, dismounted to escape through a nearby ravine, but were captured by the British to a total of one lieutenant colonel, two majors and 96 other ranks.

On August 12, 1812 the helmet was introduced, and the white facings changed to blue.

The 4th (Royal Irish) Dragoon Guards wore the blue facings proper to a Royal regiment. They too were raised in 1685 as 'Arran's Cuirassiers', and became the 4th Dragoon Guards in 1788.

They arrived in Portugal on April 4, 1811, and on January 19, 1812, were brigaded with the 3rd Dragoon Guards and the 1st (Royal) Dragoons. In the same year they replaced their cocked hats by the new helmet (Fig 3) and took sabretaches into wear. They did little active fighting, however, and were ordered home, with the 9th, 11th and 13th Light Dragoons, in 1813, after having transferred their horses to the 1st Dragoons and 3rd Dragoon Guards.

The 5th Dragoon Guards (Fig 4) at a strength of 6 troops (546 all ranks) arrived at Lisbon on September 4, 1811. In April 1812, after a forced march of 60 miles, the Regiment attacked a force three times its number of French cavalry at Llerena, and, in company with the Light Brigade, put them to flight.

Salamanca, on the other hand, started badly for the 5th. There had been a bad thunder storm on the previous night and twenty men were disabled by frightened horses, many of which stampeded and escaped. But during the battle, the Regiment, brigaded with the 3rd and 4th Dragoons repulsed 1200 French infantry, and in that action the 5th captured the staff of the drum major of the French 66th Infantry Regiment. This trophy is still in the possession of the Regiment and is paraded on ceremonial occasions in the hands of the trumpet-major.

At Toulouse the 5th was instrumental in saving the Portuguese guns from capture, and on the conclusion of hostilities moved to Boulogne, where it handed over a number of horses for mounting the newly-formed Royal Guard of Louis XVIII.

DRAGOONS

These troops, when they were first formed in the late 17th century, were really mounted infantry. Their horses served merely as vehicles to convey them to the scene of fighting, where they dismounted and went into action on foot.

There were three of these regiments in the Peninsula: the 1st, 3rd and 4th. The 1st (Royal Dragoons) were not originally raised as Dragoons, but as a troop of cuirassiers in 1661, when Charles II married Catherine of Braganca, who brought with her the territory of Tangier as part of her dowry. The Regiment was therefore sent to help garrison that possession, and for some time was known as the 'Tangier Cuirassiers'.

The 1st Royal Dragoons (Fig 5) disembarked at Lisbon on 12th and 13th September 1809 and took part in a rather tragi-comical affair at Lleira on June 11, 1812. The Dragoons were cooking their meal when suddenly the French 17th and 27th Dragoons were reported in sight. The Royals and 3rd Dragoons Guards immediately formed and charged, capturing one of General l'Allemand's ADCs; but some French reserves then appeared unexpectedly, to the confusion of both sides, who promptly turned and ran away from each other. Captain Hutton of the Royals rallied the reserve squadron, but was unsupported by the others and therefore failed to regain the initiative.

The 3rd, originally 'The Queen Consort's Regiment of Dragoons', was raised in 1685 from three troops from the Royals, and was first stationed in Ireland, where it took part in the battle of the Boyne. After such actions as Dettingen, Culloden and the Walcheren expedition, the Regiment arrived at Lisbon in late August 1811, to be brigaded with the 5th Dragoon Guards and 4th Dragoons. It had little opportunity to distinguish itself, however, on account of the unsuitable nature of the terrain for cavalry manoeuvring; but it certainly acquired the battle-honours of 'Salamanca', 'Vittoria' and 'Toulouse'.

A painting by Denis Dighton in the Royal collection at Windsor shows a Dragoon of this regiment wearing the 1812 helmet surmounted by the crest which was replaced soon afterwards by the horsehair streamer at the back

The 10th Light Dragoons ('The Prince of Wales's Own') was one of the regiments which changed its style (and later its title) to Hussars during the course of the Peninsular War. The shabraque is crimson with white lacing, the overalls are white, the jacket dark blue, and the lacing is white or silver braid (A. H. Bowling collection).

(Fig 6). The blue and red colouring of the crest is most unusual since that ornament was usually black.

The 4th Dragoons, raised by James II after Sedgemoor as Princess Anne of Denmark's Regiment of Dragoons, fought its first major action at Dettingen in 1743, but in the Peninsula the situation was once more a question of coping with unsuitable country. Nevertheless, the 4th acquitted themselves well and earned the battle-honours of 'Talavera', 'Albuhera', 'Salamanca', 'Vittoria' and 'Toulouse'.

The Dragoon Guards and Dragoons were dressed very similarly, the only difference being that the former wore a broken line in their lace (Figs 3 and 4), and in the latter the line was continuous (Fig 6).

LIGHT DRAGOONS

Although troops of light horse had been attached for some years to the British cavalry regiments, it was not until the second half of the 18th century that they were organised in any substantial numbers and formed into separate regiments.

They were clothed in blue jackets and handsome black leather helmets covered with a large bearskin crest: the 'Tarleton helmet' which survived in the Royal Horse Artillery until after Waterloo. The jackets had collar and cuffs in the regimental facing colour, and the front was covered with hussar-type lacing, while white breeches and light boots completed a very smart and businesslike outfit.

Eight Light Dragoon Regiments were engaged in the Peninsular War at various times: the 9th, 11th, 12th, 13th, 14th, 16th, 20th and 23rd. Four other regiments were there as well, but they were styled Hussars and are dealt with under that heading.

The 9th, originally a Dragoon regiment raised in 1715, was converted to Light Dragoons in 1783 (Fig 8). It sailed for the Peninsula in 1811 and was brigaded with the 13th Light Dragoons and 2nd Hussars of the King's German Legion. The regiment captured General Brune at Arroyo dos Molinos, but was ordered back to England in the spring of 1813.

Another regiment raised in 1715 was the 11th. In April 1811, at a strength of 8 troops it embarked at Portsmouth and landed at Lisbon on May 31, of that year. It was in action against French cavalry at El Bodon on September 25, 1811, and at Salamanca was in the lead of the pursuit after the battle. Early in 1813, however, it was returned to England, having lost over 400 men and 500 horses.

The 12th Light Dragoons was one of the regiments in which the future Duke of Wellington served as a young officer, in this case from 1789 to 1791. In 1811 it arrived at Lisbon, to be brigaded with the 1st (Royal) Dragoons; and it was in the Peninsula that the custom arose for the band to play hymns every evening. The origin of the tradition is a little obscure, some saying that it was a punishment for breaking into a monastery, and others that the music was simply presented to the regiment by Pope Pius VI, on a visit to Italy in 1793, with the request that it be added to the band's usual repertoire.

Yet another 1715 regiment was the 13th Light Dragoons, who were so continuously engaged in the Peninsula that they became known as the 'Ragged Brigade'. They arrived at Lisbon on May 28, 1810, five troops going to Cadiz in April and the remainder proceeding to the front in May and June.

In the following year the regiment was at Arroyo dos Molinos; in 1812 it was in the British retirement; in 1813 at Vittoria, and in 1814 in the long march to Boulogne. Further battle-honours were 'Albuhera', 'Otthes' and 'Toulouse', and in all it participated in no less than 32 actions, losing 276 men and 1,000 horses.

The 14th, too, was very active in the war. Raised in 1715, it was numbered 14th in 1798 and given the Prussian Eagle as a badge, in honour of Frederica Charlotte, Princess of Prussia and wife of the Duke of York.

It disembarked at Lisbon as early as December 23, 1808, and after a number of other engagements found itself at Fuentes d'Onoro, where a squadron under Captain Brotherton rode out to assist Norman Ramsay in his famous Horse Artillery gallop (see under Artillery). Not only that, but the squadron also captured General Lamotte as well.

However the regiment's most treasured and light hearted capture was King Joseph's travelling chamber-pot. After the battle of Vittoria, the King was making his escape when his carriage was overtaken by a detachment of the 14th. He managed to scramble out and make off on horseback, just in time. The 14th lost their quarry but found a very useful utensil; and although a chamber-pot cannot compare with a king, the trophy still graces the officers' mess in solemn dignity.

For the 16th Light Dragoons, the Peninsular War was the second occasion on which it went to Portugal, the first being in 1762, three years after its raising, in the war against Spain.

In 1766 it acquired the title of the 16th or 'The Queen's Regiment of Light

Dragoons', and sailed for Portugal in 1809. Its service in the Peninsula was long and unbroken, and it fought in most of the major battles. It did not return to England until July 1814 (Fig 12).

Finally, the 23rd Light Dragoons (Fig 11) had a rather confusing history, since there were two regiments of the same arm bearing that number. Previously numbered the 19th, the regiment had been the 23rd originally, a number which it re-claimed later. It was badly cut up at Talavera, and its lost helmets, strewn about the battlefield, were appropriated by the musicians of the Baden contingent and worn by them for the rest of the campaign.

The following facings and lacings were worn by these seven Light Dragoon regiments at this period:

Regiment	Lace	Facings
9th	gold	—
11th	silver	chamois (light brown)
12th	silver	yellow
13th	gold	chamois (light brown)
14th	silver	orange
16th	silver	scarlet
20th	silver	yellow
23rd	silver	crimson

HUSSARS

In Great Britain the Hussars were formed entirely from existing units of light dragoons, and were not officially so described until the Authorities felt compelled to recognise the *fait accompli* of some colonels—including the Prince of Wales—who took it upon themselves to equip their regiments as Hussars.

All four regiments were active in the Peninsula, and Figs 8, 9 and 10 show the three different types of head-dress in wear at that period. The earliest was the *mirliton* or *flügelmütze,* much in vogue in the 7th, followed by the tall fur busby favoured of the 10th. However, this 'monstrous muff' (as it had been termed by a critical MP) was distinctly unpopular, being top-heavy and prone to fall off. Therefore several regiments preferred a more secure cap for active service and there is evidence that the 10th and 15th were issued with scarlet shakos in January 1813 (Fig 10).

The 7th Light Dragoons, formed from independent companies as long ago as 1689, was disbanded for a few years in the early 18th century but re-raised in 1715 under the title of 'Her Royal Highness the Princess of Wales's Own Regiment of Dragoons'. In 1727 the Princess became Queen, so the regiment was styled, more simply 'The Queen's Own' before becoming the 7th in 1751. After fighting at Warburg in 1759 it became a light dragoon unit and finally acquired its hussar status at the turn of the 18th century. In the Peninsula it was heavily engaged at Orthes and Wellington makes repeated mention of its distinguished conduct on that occasion.

The 10th was raised in 1745 and became 'The Prince of Wales's Own' in 1783 when the King's eldest son became Colonel of the regiment. It was he, in fact, who first dressed his regiment as hussars, thus setting an extravagant fashion for others to follow (Fig 9).

Although the 10th did no spectacular deeds of valour in the Peninsula, it nevertheless helped to cover the retreat to Corunna, and at Benevento ambushed a French force, driving it into the river. It was also specially mentioned for its 'gallant and steady conduct at Orthes and Toulouse'.

The 15th Light Dragoons became Hussars in 1806, after an excellent record of distinguished service, particularly at Emsdorf in 1760, where it captured 9 pairs of Colours, 5 guns and 1 howitzer. The fact was first recorded in a lengthy battle-honour worn on the head-dress, but this was soon replaced by the device of crossed flags reversed, appearing in the corner of the shabraque.

Finally, the 18th, raised in 1759, was converted to Hussars in 1805. It had a short tour of duty in Ireland before embarking at Northfleet and arriving at Montego Bay on August 21, 1808, some 730 strong (Figs 12 and 13).

However, no spectacular deeds were performed, although this regiment is yet another to claim the future Duke of Wellington among its former officers, since he served with it just before joining the 33rd Foot.

ARTILLERY

The Horse Artillery was only 15 years old at the start of the Peninsular War, formed as a result of the need for mobile artillery to support the movements of cavalry. All personnel were mounted, and the uniform was modelled on the Light Dragoons.

The outstanding action of this branch was undoubtedly Norman Ramsay's famous gallop at Fuentes de Onoro in 1811, an exploit which Napier recorded in his own inimitable style. 'The French', he wrote, 'with one shock drove all the cavalry outguards, and cutting Captain Ramsay's battery, came sweeping in upon the reserves of horses . . . and at the same time a great commotion was observed in the main body. Men and horses then closed in confusion and tumult to one point, a thick dust arose, and loud cries and the sparkling of blades, and the flashing of pistols, indicated some extraordinary occurrence. Suddenly . . . an English shout pealed high and clear . . . and Norman Ramsay burst forth at the head of his battery, his horses breathing fire, stretched like greyhounds along the plain, the guns bounding behind like things of no weight

ROYAL HORSE ARTILLERY 1804-15
Gunner, 1812
HELMET: White plume. Blue turban. Brass fittings.
JACKET: Blue. Scarlet collar, cuffs, shoulder-straps. Yellow lacing. Brass buttons.
BREECHES, BELT, GLOVES: White
HORSE-FURNITURE: Blue, edged red. Blue blankets (rolled).
(after Goddard "Mil. Cost. Eur." and Hamilton Smith)

ROYAL HORSE ARTILLERY 1804-15
Corporal, 1814
HELMET: White plume. Blue turban. Brass fittings.
JACKET: Blue. Scarlet collar and cuffs. Yellow lacing and chevrons. Brass buttons.
OVERALLS: Grey. Scarlet stripes.
BELT, SLINGS: White.
SWORD: All-steel. White knot.
(after Denis Dighton, in Reynolds MSS)

ROYAL REGT. OF ARTILLERY 1801-15
Officer, 1804
HAT: White plume. Gold ornaments.
COAT: Blue. Scarlet collar, cuffs, piping. White turnbacks. Gold epaulettes and buttons.
GLOVES, BELT, BREECHES: White.
SASH: Crimson. SWORD: Gilt fittings.
(after Macdonald, "Dress ... of R.A.")

ROYAL REGT. OF ARTILLERY 1801-15
Gunner, 1801
CAP: White-over-red plume. Brass plate. Powdered hair.
JACKET: Blue. Scarlet collar, shoulder-straps, cuffs. White turnbacks. Yellow lace. Brass buttons.
BREECHES, BELTS: White. Crimson flask-cord. Brass fittings.
(after Atkinson's "Costumes")

and the mounted gunners following in full career.'

In the Foot Branch, however, things were less exciting. The Royal Artillery plodded along with the Army, perhaps a little conscious that it was controlled by the Board of Ordnance, and was not ultimately responsible to the Commander-in-Chief. Wellington, for his part, was always somewhat critical of his gunners; but Sir John Moore, on the other hand, referring to the retreat to Corunna, said, 'The Artillery consists of particularly well-behaved men'. In the 11 brigades involved there was not a single straggler.

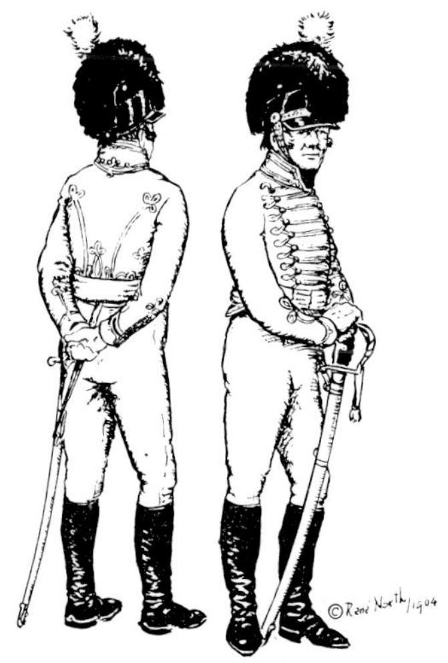

ROYAL HORSE ARTILLERY 1804-15
Officers, 1804-5
HELMETS: White plume. Gilt fittings.
JACKETS: Blue. Scarlet collar and cuffs. Gold lacing and buttons.
SASHES: Crimson and gilt.
BREECHES, GLOVES: White.
SWORDS: All-steel. Gold knot.
(after actual garments)

FOOT GUARDS

The 1st Foot Guards (Fig 23) (now the Grenadier Guards) were raised in 1657 from loyal English gentlemen who had chosen to accompany Charles II into exile, and became the senior foot regiment at the Restoration of 1660.

The regiment served in most of the subsequent campaigns, and all three battalions arrived in Spain for the Peninsular War on October 29, 1808. According to a contemporary painting of the scene, the troops were dressed in the 'stove-pipe' cap and regulation red jacket, with either white trousers or the white breeches and black gaiters issued for home wear.

They fought conspicuously at Corunna, when the remains of the British Army turned at bay, and distinguished themselves later at Barrosa and the Nive.

The 2nd (now the Coldstream Guards) were also at Barrosa, as well as Talavera, Fuentes de Onoro and the Nive, while at the end of the war, at Bayonne on August 14, 1814, they had no fewer than 156 casualties.

These same battle-honours are shared by the 3rd Foot Guards (now the Scots Guards), and at Talavera on July 27–28, 1809, an incident occurred which anticipated by over 100 years that singular Christmas truce on the Western Front in 1914. Captain Stothart, the Adjutant of the regiment, wrote that 'at about 11 a.m. the firing seemed to peter out as if by mutual consent. But British and French soldiers shook hands with each other and expressed their admiration of the gallantry displayed by the troops of both nations.'

The Foot Guards wore the dark blue facings of Royal regiments, and the individual regiments were distinguished by the setting of the buttons on their jackets—the 1st equally spaced; the 2nd in pairs, and the 3rd in threes—arrangements still in force to-day. In addition, the loops were bastion-shaped in the 2nd and pointed in the other two. Bandsmen had their tunic colours reversed—ie, dark blue tunics with red facings (Fig 24).

INFANTRY OF THE LINE

The number of Line regiments which took part in the campaign is obviously so large that no detailed survey can be made here. However, their dress can be summarised as follows:

Regiment	Facings	Loops	Officers' Lace
1st	blue	square, pairs	gold
2nd	blue	square, singles	silver
3rd	buff	square, pairs	silver
4th	blue	bastion, singles	silver
5th	Gosling green	bastion, singles	silver
6th	yellow	square, pairs	silver
7th	blue	square, singles	gold
9th	light yellow	square, pairs	silver
11th	green	bastion, pairs	gold
14th	buff	square, pairs	silver
20th	yellow	square, pairs	silver
23rd	blue	bastion, singles	gold
24th	green	square, pairs	silver
26th	yellow	bastion, singles	silver
27th	buff	square, singles	gold
28th	yellow	square, pairs	silver
29th	yellow	square, pairs	silver
30th	light yellow	bastion, singles	silver
31st	dark buff	square, singles	silver

Regiment	Facings	Loops	Officers' Lace
32nd	white	square, pairs	gold
34th	yellow	square, pairs	silver
36th	green	square, pairs	gold
38th	yellow	bastion, singles	silver
39th	green	square, pairs	silver
40th	buff	square, pairs	gold
44th	yellow	square, singles	silver
45th	green	bastion, pairs	silver
47th	white	square, pairs	silver
48th	buff	square pairs,	gold
50th	black	square, pairs	silver
57th	buff	square pairs,	gold
58th	black	square, singles	gold
59th	white	bastion, singles	gold
61st	dark buff	square, singles	silver
62nd	green	square, pairs	silver
66th	green	square, singles	silver
68th	green	square, pairs	silver
76th	red	square, pairs	silver
77th	yellow	square, singles	silver
80th	yellow	pointed, pairs	gold
81st	buff	pointed, pairs	silver
82nd	yellow	bastion, pairs	silver
83rd	yellow	square, pairs	gold
84th	yellow	square, pairs	silver
87th	green	pointed, pairs	gold
88th	yellow	pointed, pairs	silver
89th	black	pointed, pairs	gold
90th	buff	square, pairs	gold
91st	yellow	square pairs,	silver
94th	green	square, pairs	gold
97th	yellow	pointed, singles	silver

Officers' loops were always square-ended and their epaulettes were in the same metal as the lace.

It will be seen from the above table that some of these regiments were dressed exactly alike, but since the regimental lace (on the collar and forming the loops on the jacket) was always of regimental pattern, some measure of distinction was thereby preserved. Further all regiments with buff facings wore buff breeches as well.

Those units which started out early in the campaign were naturally wearing the 'stove-pipe' shako and the clubbed hair which was abolished on August 1, 1808, and although the 'belgic' shako was authorised in 1811, it is reasonable to suppose that issues did not reach the units in the field until much later.

It would be invidious to single out a particular regiment, when so many fought with such gallantry but one cannot help thinking of the 57th (later The Middlesex Regiment) whose magnificent stand at Albuhera on May 16, 1811 remains a classic of military victory. Greatly outnumbered, the 57th withstood a terrible fire of shell and grapeshot, holding a hill which they had captured against a column more than four times their number. Colonel Inglis, the commanding officer, was mortally wounded, but he rallied his regiment by calling out, 'Die hard, my men; die hard!' Out of 570 all ranks, 430 were dead

BRITISH LINE INFANTRY

These two views show typical men of British line infantry regiments. Basically the uniform was standard for all regiments, the main distinctions being in the facing colours (collars and cuffs) and the grouping and style of the lace. On the left can be seen square loops in pairs while the man on the right has single loops with bastion ends. Man on left is in parade dress with white trousers and gaiters; on the right is campaign dress with grey overalls. Note the clubbed hair style on right, abolished in 1808.

or wounded; and the 57th earned itself the proud nickname of 'The Diehards'.

Indeed, the British infantry in general received universal admiration. Marshal Soult, in generous appreciation, said, 'There is no beating these troops, in spite of their generals; . . . they were everywhere broken, the day was mine, and yet they did not know it, and would not run'. (Fig 23)

HIGHLANDERS

Of the six Highland regiments employed in the Peninsula, only three were kilted, because the 71st and 74th were a light infantry unit; later to become The Highland Light Infantry, and the 91st did not have its Highland dress restored until 1881.

This, then, leaves the 42nd, 79th and 92nd, better known in later years respectively as The Black Watch, The Queen's Own Cameron Highlanders and the 2nd Battalion The Gordons. The 42nd—the only Highland regiment to wear a red hackle—was formed in 1730 from a number of independent companies of Scottish gentlemen whose duty was to keep order in the Highlands. One of their responsibilities was to suppress the collection of 'black meal', a highly illegal levy imposed by marauding Highlanders and often demanded

The 57th Foot, in campaign dress, march past their colonel shortly before the Battle of Albuhera where their gallant stand earned them the nickname of 'The Diehards'.

with menaces. The term has passed into current speech as 'blackmail' and the Government troops became the 'Black Watch'. Indeed the sombre sett of their tartan is often referred to as 'Government' pattern, and some authorities maintain that the name simply refers to the colour of the kilt.

In the Peninsula, the 42nd won no less than eight battle-honours: 'Corunna', 'Busaco', 'Fuentes de Onoro', 'Pyrenees', 'Nivelle', 'Nive', 'Orthes and 'Toulouse'.

The 79th was raised by Cameron of Erracht in 1793: the same year, incidentally, as the Royal Horse Artillery. A remarkably tough regiment, this, for when it had 700 all ranks down with typhus after the retreat to Corunna, not a single man died; and even after the disastrous Walcheren expedition was able to return intact to Spain to resume the campaign. Here it won the same battle-honours as the 42nd, except that 'Salamanca' replaced 'Orthes',

The 92nd dates from 1794 and saw considerable fighting in Europe while the 1st Batalion of the Gordons—the 75th Foot—was serving in India, Its seven Peninsula battle-honours were: 'Corunna', 'Fuentes de Onoro', 'Almarez', 'Vittoroa', 'Pyrenees', 'Nive' and 'Orthes'.

All three regiments took part later in the Waterloo campaign and distinguished themselves both at Quatre Bras and at La Haye Sainte.

THE BLACK WATCH

The officer (left) wears the red double-breasted coatee with gold lace and dark blue facings. The sash is crimson, the cross-belt white, and gorget silver. The sergeant (right) has white lace, gold chevrons, the hackle being red. He carries a halfpike.

LIGHT INFANTRY

The seven Light Infantry regiments in the Peninsular War were dressed in the regulation red jacket, with distinctions as follows:

Regiment	Facings	Loops	Officers' Lace
43rd	white	square, pairs	silver
51st	green	pointed, pairs	gold
52nd	buff	square, pairs	silver
53rd	red	square, pairs	gold
71st	buff	square, singles	silver
74th	white	square, singles	gold
85th	yellow	square, pairs	silver

The cap was of the conical variety peculiar to the light infantry, and the shoulders carried the 'wings' which proclaimed light troops. The 53rd, however, may have been an exception, for a contemporary, though rather primitive sketch in the regimental museum at Shrewsbury shows a certain Sergeant Mosley wearing a 'belgic' shako, and instead of wings a pair of shoulder-straps in the form of fringeless epaulettes.

The first substantial organisation of Light Infantry was carried out by Sir John Moore, the hero of Corunna, after he had studied the French system of dividing a battalion into skirmishers, supports and reserves. He tried out the system in his own regiment, the 52nd, and at a later date a number of other units adopted the same procedure.

In the Peninsula the 52nd was brigaded with the 43rd and the Rifle Brigade to form that dauntless Light Brigade which performed such astonishing achievements while covering the retreat to Corunna. In fact, the 43rd and 52nd between them won a total of thirteen battle honours in the campaign.

The 51st (later to become The King's Own Yorkshire Light Infantry) was raised in 1756 and also helped in that rearguard action; and the 53rd, gaining eight battle honours, subsequently fought at Waterloo. After Napoleon's surrender, it watched over him at St Helena, and the Emperor often made appreciative remarks on its conduct.

Scotland was represented by the 71st and 74th Light Infantry (the 1st and 2nd Battalions of The Highland Light Infantry), but in their case the cap was dark blue and bore the traditional dice-border around the base. These two regiments wore the regulation breeches and trousers of the British infantry, but the former were buff in colour to conform with the buff facings. The pipers, of course, were kilted.

These two regiments beat even the 43rd and 52nds' record, by achieving no less than fifteen Peninsular battle-honours in all.

The 85th later became the 2nd Battalion The King's Shropshire Light Infantry (53rd Foot) and shared in winning the battle-honours mentioned above.

RIFLE REGIMENTS

Both Rifle regiments of the British army, the 60th and the 95th were very active in the Peninsular War.

These troops were a comparatively new departure, arising as they did from the necessity for producing extra-light infantry as an antidote to the American rangers in the War of Independence. Accordingly, the 5th Battalion of the 60th Foot (The Royal Americans) was clothed in dark green, equipped with Baker

(continued on page 22)

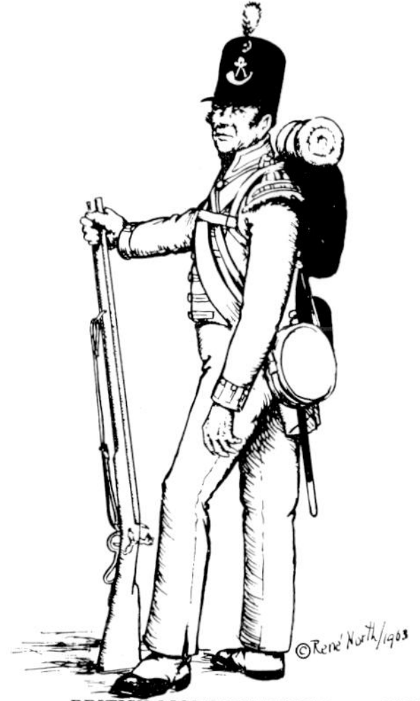

BRITISH LIGHT INFANTRY 1811-15
Private, 85th Regt., c.1814
CAP: Green plume. Brass badge.
JACKET: Red. Yellow collar, shoulder-straps, cuffs. White lace, turnbacks, belts. Pewter buttons.
TROUSERS, GAITERS: Blue-grey.
EQUIPMENT: Blue water-bottle. Grey greatcoat. Brass-tipped scabbard.
(after Reynolds MSS)

BRITISH RIFLE REGIMENTS 1800-12
Rifleman, 95th Foot, 1806
CAP: White-over-green plume. Green lines.
JACKET: Dark green. White lace and powder-horn. In front, three rows of silver buttons.
BREECHES: Dark green. White piping.
SWORD: Brass fittings.
(from Reynolds MSS after Atkinson)

(1) Royal Horse Guards, Officer. (2) 3rd Dragoon Guards, 1812. (3) 4th Dragoon Guards, Trooper, 1813. (4) 5th Dragoon Guards, Trooper, 1812. (5) 1st Royal Dragoons, Trooper, 1810. (6) 3rd Royal Dragoons, Trooper, 1812. (7) 4th Dragoons, Trooper. (8) 9th Light Dragoons, Officer, 1811. (9) 10th Light Dragoons, Trooper. (10) 15th Light Dragoons, Trooper, 1813.

(11) 23rd Light Dragoons, Trooper, 1812. (12) 18th Light Dragoons, 1809. (13) 18th Light Dragoons, 1813. (14) 30th Foot, Private. (15) Royal Corps of Sappers and Miners, Sergeant. (16) Royal Waggoners, Officer. (17) Surgeon. (18) King's German Legion Hussars, Officer. (19) King's German Legion, Heavy Dragoon. (20) King's German Legion, Infantry.

BRITISH RIFLE REGIMENTS 1800-12
Officer, 60th Foot, c.1808
JACKET: Dark green. Red collar (red loop). Dark green loops. Silver lace and buttons.
WINGS: Silver, lined red.
BREECHES: Grey.
SASH: Crimson.
(after actual garment)

BRITISH RIFLE REGIMENTS 1800-12
Officer, 60th Foot, 1812
CAP: Green plume. Silver bugle.
JACKET: Dark green. Red collar, cuffs, lapels. Silver lace, buttons, wings (lined red).
BELT: White. Silver plate.
SASH: Crimson.
SWORD: Gilt fittings.
(from Reynolds MSS)

rifles and trained intensively in skirmishing, fieldcraft and scouting. The soldier was taught to think for himself and act on his own initiative: a revolutionary concept in those days.

The experiment proved so successful that a second corps was raised. Men were transferred from 15 existing regiments and formed into the Rifle Corps which, in August 1800, was numbered 95th Foot. The name was later changed to The Rifle Brigade, while the 60th became The King's Royal Rifle Corps, the main distinction between the two being the red facings of the 60th and the black ones of the 95th (Fig 21).

The Baker rifle, a much more accurate weapon than the musket, was considerably shorter than the latter and was grooved inside the bore, exactly like a present-day rifle, thus imparting a spin to the bullet which greatly increased its efficiency. The short barrel of the rifle made it eminently suitable for action in wooded country, but it was not designed to take a bayonet. The riflemen used their short straight swords in that capacity, and even to-day the order is always given as 'fix swords!' rather than 'fix bayonets!'

The rifle regiments, in fact, have a number of other proud and respected traditions. For instance, they march at the rapid pace of 140 steps to the minute; they have no drums or colours; they never slope arms, but proceed at the trail or the shoulder, and their rifle-slings always hang loose. There are probably many more customs which are cherished by those highly distinctive regiments, whose exploits and sufferings in the Peninsula are graphically described in the memoirs of Rifleman Harris, the shepherd boy from Blandford, who went through the whole campaign unhurt, only to be discharged afterwards following a long attack of Walcheren fever.

ENGINEERS

Military engineering, transport and medical services: these and the commissariat are the main departments that keep an army functioning smoothly in war as well as in peace.

A private (left) and officer of the 95th Foot in the dark green of the rifle regiments. The facings (collars and cuffs) are black, as are the belts. The officer's waist sash is crimson. Note the hussar style officer's dress with the distinctive conical mirliton cap. Private has a Baker rifle and short sword (A. H. Bowling collection).

In 1813 the engineering branch consisted of two separate bodies: the Royal Engineers, a corps of specialist officers, with the Royal Corps of Sappers and Miners forming the rank-and-file of the organisation. The R.E., originally in a blue coat, cocked hat, and blue trousers, were soon afterwards dressed in scarlet because they were sometimes mistaken for French Officers. For the Sappers and Miners the uniform was basically that of the Royal Artillery in reversed colours, and the distinctive round cap shown in Fig 15 was no doubt an undress type of head-dress worn when troops were engaged on field works. The initials R.S.M., incidentally, denote the corps and not a superior rank of warrant-officer!

(21) King's German Legion, Light Infantry and 95th Foot. (22) K.G.L. Infantry, Light Company. (23) 1st Foot Guards. (24) 2nd Foot Guards, drummer. (25) Veterinary Surgeon, 1809. (26) Spanish Toledo Regiment. (27) Portuguese Dragoons, Officer. (28) 11th Bn, Portuguese Cacadors, 1811. (29) Loyal Lusitanian Legion. (30) Chasseur of the Guard, full dress.

(31) Chasseur of the Guard, Campaign Dress. (32) Polish Lancer of the Guard. (33) 26th Chasseurs à Cheval. (34) 1st Hussars. (35) 2nd Hussars. (36) 3rd Hussars. (37) Lanciers de Berg. (38) Gendarmes-Chevaulegers. (39) Fusilier-Grenadiers of the Guard. (40) Chasseurs of the Guard.

TRANSPORT

The transport was in the hands of a department as long-suffering as its own pack-animals, constantly re-named, and at this time known as The Royal Waggon Train. It was previously called the Royal Waggoners, and when it assumed its new title in 1799 it was clothed in blue. In 1811, however, the colour of the jacket was changed to red (Fig 16) and while the officers wore a cocked hat, the other ranks were issued with whatever type of shako was in vogue at the moment. By 1814 there were 14 troops in existence, with a total strength of 1,904 rank-and-file.

During the Peninsular War the transport branch depended upon the Commissariat under Sir John Bissett. However, at the beginning of hostilities Wellington rather unwisely relied too much on Spanish promises to supply the army's needs. Thus, little victualling was done from home, and when the Spanish authorities not only denied, but actively hindered the provision of food and fodder, things became serious indeed.

Fodder was virtually non-existent, and 1500 horses and mules died from starvation. As for the men, in 1809 their rations amounted to no more than $\frac{1}{2}$lb of bread and a few ounces of flour every day, plus $\frac{1}{4}$lb of goat's meat once a week. The rest had to be found 'on the country', a procedure highly detrimental to discipline and very conducive to corrupt practices.

Even such essential commodities as waggons were refused; but on the other hand pack mules were easily obtained and 10,000 of these animals were added to those already in the regimental transport sections.

That, of course, did not solve the problem, and Bissett therefore thought out a new type of bullock-cart with iron axle-trees and brass boxes. Eight hundred of these were produced eventually, and their presence had a marked effect on the future conduct of the war.

In March 1810 the officers were given military rank, although remaining Treasury officials as before, as follows:

The Commissary-General became a Brigadier General; a Deputy became a Major (and after 3 years a Lieutenant Colonel); an Assistant was a Captain; a Deputy-Assistant a Lieutenant, and a Clerk an Ensign.

By 1811 nearly all Deputy Assistants had acquired some experience in the field, which while perhaps not improving their Civil Service status, at any rate gave them the confidence to exercise that very necessary military virtue of improvisation. Nevertheless, a Commissary's task was difficult, controlled as he was by a distant Treasury with no appreciation of the requirements of an army on active service. Wellington, however, was sympathetic and did all he could to improve the service. He knew, as well as his illustrious opponent, that 'an army marches on its stomach'. Even so, the Commissariat Department in the Peninsula was by no means over strength, 719 men all told, practising a number of diverse trades. Strangely enough they included only one farrier, but 13 interpreters.

MEDICAL AND VETERINARY SERVICES

In the harsh days of Napoleonic warfare the medical service was disgracefully primitive and, one feels, rather unwanted. A man was supposed to be either fit or dead: if he was wounded he became a liability.

This callous attitude, fortunately, became more humane chiefly through the efforts of Sir James McGrigor, the Inspector of Hospitals, and George Guthrie, the surgeon of the 29th Foot. They were working on the foundations laid in the 18th century by Sir John Pringle and John Hunter, but despite their efforts the

Army in the Peninsula was still short of medical personnel and supplies. In 1808 there were only two bullock-drawn ambulances for the whole army, although every regiment had its own pack-mule and cart. But the mule served to carry the surgeon's panniers and the cart was used for the wounded mens' accoutrements. The casualties themselves were transported in rough, unsprung ox-carts, receiving scant attention and not much to eat. Little wonder that typhus was a frequent epidemic.

The medical orderlies, instead of being men trained in hospital duties, were simply details from sundry regiments: very often the indifferent soldiers whom commanding officers were anxious to get rid of. The fact that so many men came through the retreat to Corunna is a tribute not so much to the skill of the medical service, as to the robust constitution of the survivors.

In spite of Wellington's indifference, McGrigor went ahead with his plans, establishing a chain of hospitals all along the route to Salamanca and using Commissariat transport to evacuate the wounded from the battlefield. He also arranged for the wooden framework of huts to be sent out from England (an early instance of prefabricated structures), and finally assembled a village for as many as 400 sick. He then set to work, engaging French and Spanish doctors to help in his task, and finally sent back some 5,000 men to their units. The astonishing fact had at last emerged that the sick and wounded could be cured.

The officers of the Medical Department did not wear the crimson sash, nor did they in many cases carry a sword. They were distinguished by a system of buttons and loops, as follows:

Inspector: two gold epaulettes and two gold loops on the collar. Deputy Inspector: two epaulettes, but one loop only. Physician: the same, but no loop. Surgeon: as Physician, but no epaulettes (Fig 17).

The Veterinary Service was even worse off than the Medical; for example during the whole of 1810, the Royal Artillery had no veterinary surgeon at all. Normally, there was one of these officers attached to every cavalry regiment, but in the artillery never more than two vets were present together: presumably one for the Horse branch and one for the Foot. Like other departmental officers the veterinary surgeon wore a tricorne hat and scarlet coat (Fig 25).

Wellington, who described Spain as 'the grave of horses' made every endeavour to improve the situation. He finished the campaign with 24 veterinary surgeons in his army, which included 10 for the cavalry, one for the Cavalry Staff Corps, two for the Artillery, one for the Waggon Train and three for the King's German Legion—a truly pitiful number for an organisation so dependent on its horses.

KING'S GERMAN LEGION: LIGHT CAVALRY

During the Continental wars of 1801–6, the Kingdom of Hanover, closely associated as it was with the British Crown, found itself in an extremely uneasy position, being occupied alternately by France and Prussia. It is not surprising that attempts were soon made to regain contact with Great Britain by encouraging a more or less clandestine enlistment of recruits for the British service.

Thus, on August 10, 1803, King George III charged Baron Decken with the raising of a corps of light infantry to be called The King's Germans. By November, 450 recruits had arrived in the Isle of Wight, and as prospects seemed favourable, it was resolved to extend the establishment to cavalry and artillery as well, and to name the entire force The King's German Legion.

The first cavalry units were heavy and light dragoons: two regiments of the

(continued on page 30)

(41) Infantry of the Line. (42) Infantry of the Line in Campaign Dress. (43) Swiss Valais Regiment. (44) 7th Polish Infantry. (45) 9th Polish Infantry. (46) Nassau Cavalry. (47) Nassau Infantry. (48) Hanoverian Legion Cavalry, Trumpeter. (49) Hanoverian Legion Infantry. (50) Westphalian Chevaulegers-Lanciers.

(51) Baden Contingent Artillery. (52) Baden Contingent Infantry. (53) Baden Contingent Transport Section. (54) Spanish Grenadier Regiment (King Joseph's Guard). (55) 2nd Regiment, Cazadores à Caballo. (56) Spanish Queen's Dragoons. (57) Spanish La Mancha Lancers. (58) Frankfort Line Infantry. (59) Sailors of the Guard. (60) Westphalian Garde du Corps, 1708.

former and three of the latter. On December 28, 1813, however, the Dragoons were converted to Light Dragoons, and the three regiments of Light Dragoons became Hussars.

The general appearance of the Heavy Dragoons was very similar to that of the British Dragoon Guards of the period (Fig 19); but officers of the 2nd Regiment sometimes wore an undress cap in the form of a small busby, with peak, and a black busby-bag with a gold cord and tassel falling to the right The conventional bicorne hat was also worn, with gilt chin-scales hooked up at the back of the hat when not in wear; and the dark blue overalls are interesting in the fact that a black tassel ornamented the front of the black leather false boots (only about 6 inches high).

On August 11, 1812, the Dragoons were in action at Majadahonda, while on the march to Madrid. The German Division was ahead of the main body, but the vanguard had hastened back with the news that the enemy under Treilhard had turned. The trumpeters immediately sounded the alarm, but the troops, unsaddled for the first time in three days, were either washing or watering their horses. However, two companies of light infantry and two small bodies of Dragoons were able to check the first onslaught and give time for the remainder to mount; but it was then that the Portuguese infantry turned tail, forcing the Dragoons to fall back on Rozas, losing their Brigadier, de Joncquières, in the retirement. However, they re-formed and charged, and as Ponsonby approached with reinforcements, Treilhard and his Frenchmen drew off.

The Heavy Dragoons had a pair of kettle drums for ceremonial occasions, and a band of 8 musicians and 8 trumpeters under a trumpet-major, but unfortunately no description of their dress has come to light.

KING'S GERMAN LEGION: HUSSARS

The Hussars were formed from the three regiments of Light Dragoons, and in 1811 the 1st regiment (Fig 18) was in Arentschild's Brigade of Cettow's Division, while at Salamanca it was brigaded with the 14th Light Dragoons under von Alten.

The 2nd Hussars sustained heavy losses while they were operating with the British 11th and 13th Light Dragoons, but they had their revenge at Arroyo dos Molinos when they captured 200 prisoners. But as a general rule the German hussars were employed chiefly on reconnaissance and escort duties, because for some reason the commanders seem to have preferred them, for these services, to the British cavalry.

The 2nd Hussars were dressed much as the 1st, but with white collars and cuffs. Officers wore a brown fur busby with a black leather peak (ornaments as in the 1st), grey overalls, and a gold girdle with two crimson stripes. The fur on the pelisse was white.

K.G.L.: INFANTRY AND LIGHT INFANTRY

The infantry of the K.G.L. was dressed almost the same as British (Fig 20) except that in their case the facings were dark blue for all battalions. These consisted of 10 companies each (including the grenadier and light companies), of 111 men of all ranks, which meant that after making allowance for drummers, bandsmen, orderlies and such-like personnel, the actual fighting strength, with NCOs, was reduced to about 90 men. The skirmishers, or sharpshooters, were probably peculiar to the Hanoverians—platoons of picked men (1 officer, 2 sergeants, 2 corporals, 1 bugler and 52 privates) armed with rifles and sword-bayonets as opposed to the muskets of the line units. They also had minor distinctions in their uniform.

In the Peninsula all the sharpshooter platoons were amalgamated into one unit, but in 1811 those of the light battalions were returned to their parent units.

Each Line Battalion carried a King's Colour and a Regimental Colour. The King's Colour was of course the universal Union Flag, but the Regimental Colour, in regulation pattern, was dark blue (to conform with the facings) with a small Union in the upper canton next to the staff. In the centre the battalion numeral appeared below the words 'King's German Legion' and the whole was encircled by the usual flowered wreath in full colours.

The two battalions of Light Infantry (Fig 21) were almost exact replicas of the British Rifle Brigade, even to the short rifles and sword-bayonets. The buttons were silver, and the only difference between the two units was the setting of the buttons on the jacket, for in the 1st Battalion they were placed in one central row of twelve, in the 2nd there was one additional row on each side, running from the shoulders to the waist.

The officers of the 1st Battalion wore the same conical cap as the men, but their wings were of the all-silver variety common to the British infantry officers. In the 2nd Battalion, however, the pattern was somewhat different. The head-dress was a black 'Flügelmütze' or mirliton, a peculiar article much favoured by the early hussars, and resembling, in this case, a regulation conical cap without a peak.

The jacket, in very dark green, was ornamented with black hussar braiding and the wings here were replaced by black cording along the shoulders, retained by a silver button near the collar.

All officers wore white gloves, and their sash was of the wide crimson variety, worn around the waist and terminating in crimson cords and tassels after the manner of the British light infantry.

PORTUGUESE DRAGOONS

It was unfortunate for the Portuguese cavalry, consisting entirely of Dragoons, that their blue uniform (Fig 27) was prone to cause them to be mistaken for French troops at a distance. For instance, on one occasion they were fired on heavily by the British 3rd Division and lost a number of men and horses in consequence. However, at Salamanca, the 1st and 11th Regiments, assisted by the British 14th Light Dragoons, carried out a brilliant flanking movement which took the French completely by surprise after they had repelled the main British attack.

We find them also in that action of August 11, 1812, on the road to Madrid, where they were in the vanguard of the King's German Legion Dragoons riding ahead with four guns. No specific mention is made of their contribution to the fighting, but it is an interesting point that Treilhard's Division, which was detailed to check the Allied advance, included the Lancers de Berg (Fig 38) and the Italian 'Napoleon' Dragoons.

About 1800 the Portuguese cavalry regiments were dressed in a variety of helmets, shakos and bicornes, but by 1809, when British supplies of clothing had become available, the whole branch was issued with helmets, and blue jackets with collars and cuffs in the following colours: Regiments 1 to 3, white; 4 to 6, red; 7 to 9, yellow; 10 to 12, blue. It is quite likely that the system was further elaborated within the groups of three regiments by allocating different piping colours, because four exhibits at Lisbon Museum show the following

The 13th Light Dragoons (left) in action against the French heavy dragoons in 1811 at the Battle of Albuhera.

arrangements of colours: 2nd Regiment, white facings, orange piping; 4th Regiment, red facings, white piping; 7th Regiment, orange facings, white piping; 12th Regiment, red facings, white piping. The jacket of the 12th has no shoulder-straps, which seems odd.

PORTUGUESE LINE INFANTRY

In the early stages of the war the Infantry of the Line consisted of 24 regiments, all named and numbered; and regimental distinctions were systematic rather than traditional, the variations being as follows:

Collar: First 12 regiments, blue; 13 to 15, white; 16 to 18, red; 19 to 21, yellow; and 22 to 24, light blue.

Cuffs: 1 to 3 and 13 to 15, white; 4 to 6 and 16 to 18, red; 7 to 9 and 19 to 21, yellow; 10 to 12 and 22 to 24, light blue.

Piping and lining: 1, white; 2, red; 3, yellow; then 4 white, 5 red, 6 yellow, etc, down to 24.

PORTUGUESE LINE REGIMENTS 1806-09
Grenadier, 21st (Valenca) Regt.
SHAKO: White plume; brass fittings; blue-and-yellow cords.
JACKET, TROUSERS: Blue; yellow collar, cuffs, turnbacks, piping; blue-and-yellow epaulette-fringe; brass buttons.
BELTS: White. SWORD: Brass fittings; buff knot.
POUCH: Brass numeral.
(after offl. documents, Fosten Collection)

PORTUGUESE LINE REGIMENTS 1806-09
Captain, 14th (Tavira) Regt.
SHAKO: White plume; gilt fittings; blue-and-red cords and cockade.
JACKET, BREECHES: Blue; white collar and cuffs; red turnbacks and piping; gold epaulettes and buttons.
SASH: Red. BELT: White; gilt plate.
(after offl. documents, Fosten Collection)

The Portuguese shako—probably the fore-runner of the British 'belgic' cap of 1811–12—was fitted, at the base, with a narrow brass plate bearing the regimental number in front, and above this an oval one with the Portuguese arms, while a long white plume issued from a red and blue cockade. The cords were mixed blue and lining-colour, with the addition of gold thread for all ranks above corporal. This shako was known as the 'barretinna'.

The dark blue jacket resembled the British garment in cut, and fastened with a single row of 8 brass buttons. Dark blue trousers with black gaiters were worn in winter, and white trousers in the summer.

Rank distinctions were shown by the epaulettes, which were of metal scales for all ranks down to *furriel* inclusive, while for those below that rank they consisted of blue cloth, piped in the lining colour. The various distinctions were as follows:

Colonel: Two epaulettes with large bullions.

Lieutenant-Colonel: One epaulette with bullions on the right shoulder and one without on the left.

Major: The same, but on opposite shoulders.

Captain: Two epaulettes with small fringes.

Lieutenant: As Lieutenant-Colonel, but fringe instead of bullions.

2nd Lieutenant: as Major, but fringe instead of bullions.

Sergeant: Two epaulettes with yellow worsted fringe.

2nd Sergeant/Drum Major: as Lieutenant-Colonel, but worsted fringe instead of bullions.

'Furriel': as Major, but worsted fringe instead of bullions.

Corporal: Two yellow stripes around cuffs.

Lance-Corporal: One yellow stripe around cuffs.

Grenadier: Fringe of mixed blue and lining colour; grenade on cap.

Pioneer: The same, but crossed axes on cap.

PORTUGUESE LINE REGIMENTS 1806-09
Colonel, 10th (Lisbon) Regt.
SHAKO: White plume; gilt fittings; blue-and-white cords.
JACKET, BREECHES: Blue; sky-blue cuffs; blue collar; white turnbacks and piping; gold epaulettes and buttons.
SASH: Red. BELT: White; gilt plate.
(after offl. documents, Fosten Collection)

PORTUGUESE LINE REGIMENTS 1806-09
Private, 24th (2nd Bragança) Regt.
SHAKO: White plume; brass fittings; blue-and-yellow cords; blue-and-red cockade.
JACKET, TROUSERS: Blue; sky-blue collar and cuffs; yellow turnbacks and piping; brass buttons.
BELTS: White.
(after offl. documents, Fosten Collection)

These troops were armed with a certain quantity of muskets of Portuguese origin, but the supply was inadequate. Oman informs us that at the outset of the Peninsular War only 10,000 had been issued, but by the time Wellington landed the British Government had distributed 42,000 more.

PORTUGUESE CACADORES AND LOYAL LUSITANIA LEGION

The Caçadores were established on October 14, 1808, when six battalions were raised (at a strength of 628 men each) with five companies in each, including one of *atiradores* or sharpshooters. The uniform was to be brown throughout, with facings according to the systematic Portuguese tabulation, as follows:

1st Battalion, brown collar, light blue cuffs; 2nd, brown collar, red cuffs; 3rd, brown collar, yellow cuffs. For the 4th, 5th and 6th, the collar and cuffs were, respectively, light blue, red and yellow. The piping was green, and the brass buttons corresponded with yellow loops in the British style.

White breeches or trousers were issued for summer wear, and the cap was the regulation infantry shako with a green plume for *caçadores* and black for *atiradores,* while the traditional bugle-horn appeared as a badge encircling the battalion numeral. In addition, *atiradores* wore a green fringe at the end of the epaulettes.

The loops on the jacket were gold for officers and cadets, silk for NCOs and worsted for other ranks. Epaulettes and rank badges conformed with those of the line regiments, but cornets wore musicians' lace, which was also worn by drummers and fifers, but in this case on collars and cuffs only. The lace was green and yellow for cornets, and green and white for drum majors, drummers and fifers.

A short sword was carried by cornets, drummers, fifers and other ranks, and

PORTUGUESE CAÇADORES 1808-9
Officers, 2nd and 3rd Battalions
SHAKO: Green plume and cords. Gilt fittings. Blue and red bow.
JACKETS: Brown. Red collar (2nd). Yellow collar (3rd). Gold loops, epaulettes, buttons. Green piping. Red sash. Possibly brown turnbacks.
BREECHES: White.
SWORD: Gilt fittings.
(after official documents)

PORTUGUESE CAÇADORES 1808-9
Sergeant, 4th Battalion
SHAKO: Green plume and cords. Brass fittings. Blue and red bow.
JACKET: Brown. Red collar and cuffs. Yellow loops and epaulette-fringe. Brass buttons, epaulettes, belt-plate.
BREECHES: White
SWORD: Brass fittings.
(after official documents)

was suspended from a cross-belt, which also carried the other ranks' bayonet. The latter, however, was not issued to drum majors, drummers, fifers and cornets, who were armed with pistols instead; and at this early stage, rank and file did not carry carbines, but regulation infantry muskets.

In 1811 the strength was raised to 12 battalions and the uniform altered accordingly. The brown colour was retained, but the shako was exchanged for a conical cap of British design, with the battalion numeral in brass over a bugle-horn of the same metal, and a short green plume in front. (Fig 28) The loops on the jacket were replaced by black hussar-type braiding for all battalions with three rows of black half-ball buttons, the cuffs were pointed and decorated with a black crows-foot, the shoulder-straps and wings were black also.

New facing colours were allotted on the following pattern: 1st Battalion, black collar, light blue cuffs; 2nd, black/scarlet; 3rd black/black; 4th light blue/light blue; 5th scarlet/scarlet; 6th, yellow/yellow; 7th, black/yellow; 8th, light blue/black; 9th, scarlet/black; 10th, yellow/black; 11th, light blue/scarlet; 12th, scarlet/light blue.

The Loyal Lusitanian Legion, consisting of from 2000 to 3000 Portuguese under Colonel W. Mayne earned considerable praise from British officers throughout the campaign. It is not quite clear when and where it was raised, but one of their early duties, after the British had sailed from Corunna, was to garrison the fortress of Almeida from January 5 to February 16, 1809. In early May of the same year some of the force were in action at Alcantara in company with the 11th Cavalry Regiment and Militia Regiment Idanha Nova—all under Colonel Mayne. At the Alcantara bridge, however, this small body of 1,800 men and 4 guns was overwhelmed by 12,000 Frenchmen, led by Marshal Victor in person, and naturally enough compelled to retreat.

It fought later at Puerta de Bainos and on the Agueda, but having been isolated for a long time from the main body of the army found itself in a most unenviable position. Mayne records that communications were so bad that his force had virtually no commissariat, no carts, no tents, not even a camp kettle among them—and no pay. All supplies had to be taken from the enemy.

At Albuhera, on May 15, 1811, the Legion was with the Fusilier Brigade when they were attacked by Werle's Brigade of 9 battalions. But although the French had a numerical superiority of 2 to 1, they were unable to deploy, being formed as they were in dense columns, so that under the dense fire of the Allies they finally broke and hurriedly retired.

The Legion was also present at Salamanca, on July 22, 1812, as well as at Ledesma, 6 miles further away on the Tormes, where it recaptured a number of horses and public money belonging to the Junta of Ciudad Rodrigo.

It was probably disbanded towards the end of the year, and no records have come to light of Colonel Mayne's subsequent service, if any. However, we do know that he was presented with a sword of honour by the officers of the 1st Battalion, and that the Government of Spain acknowledged the fact that the safety of Seville was ensured considerably by the operation of the Legion.

The uniform shown in Fig 29 was noted in Lisbon Military Museum and described as 'emerald' green in colour; however, it seems likely that this might originally have been a darker green which has faded in the course of time.

PORTUGUESE CAÇADORES 1808-9
Caçador, 6th Battalion

SHAKO: Green plume and cords. Brass fittings. Blue and red bow.

JACKET: Brown. Yellow collar, cuffs, loops. Green piping. Brass buttons and belt-plate. Possibly brown turnbacks.

BREECHES: White.

SWORD: Brass fittings

(after official documents)

Part 2: The French and their Allies

THE French made a worthy enemy, hard but chivalrous, and, of course, both the French and British sides faced a common enemy in the harsh conditions and the extremes of weather experienced in the Peninsula. Also, as occupiers of an alien land, they were considerably harassed by guerilla activities across their lines of communications, more so than the British. French forces came off worse in most of the big engagements due to their inferior tactics. The infantry most often attacked in column and were thus an easy target for the British who met them in line and fired on the heads of the advancing column This usually decimated the head of the column, demoralised the men behind, and made their rout a reasonably easy matter. However, the French had their share of victories and their major achievements are recorded in this section. Once again we shall consider the regiments in order of seniority.

HORSE CHASSEURS OF THE GUARD

After the *Guides de Bonaparte* had returned from Egypt at the turn of the 18th century, they were formed into a company of *Chasseurs à Cheval* of the Consular Guard on January 13, 1800. The unit subsequently reached regimental status, and when the Consular Guard became Imperial on May 18th, 1804, the regiment altered its title accordingly. It eventually attained an establishment of 8 squadrons, but was reduced to four after the First Abdication in 1814.

This unit was almost a permanent bodyguard to the Emperor, for detachments were continually on duty, night and day, in close proximity to his person. Thus, a small detachment was always present with the Imperial Staff wherever it went, in the same manner as a present-day motor-cycle escort. When the Staff halted, they took up positions as outposts on all sides, and if the Emperor dismounted, they and the staff did likewise.

Indeed, Napoleon was much attached to his Chasseurs, and his familiar green coat was simply the undress uniform of a Colonel in that regiment. For the others, the uniform suffered practically no change since its inception in the Consular Guard.

One hears little, if anything, of the Chasseur of the Guard in the Peninsula. They probably took no active part in the fighting, their duty being mainly to act as escorts to the Emperor and the Imperial Staff. The full dress uniform included breeches and tasselled boots, a sabretache in dark green, an ermine cloak of State, and 'aurore' lace (Fig 30). The service dress included grey-green pantalons, a plain leather sabretache, no plume on the busby and no state cloak (Fig 31). The Chasseurs always rode black horses.

Card 'flat' models by the author portraying the standard and escort of the Horse Chasseurs of the Guard in parade dress. The standard, topped by a brass imperial eagle, is basically a red, white and blue tri-colour adorned with the regimental battle honours and the imperial ciphers. Note that all the men ride black horses.

MAMELUKES

The centuries-old interest of France in all things oriental, and the happy knack of her army not only in welcoming Moslem soldiers, but also in designing their uniforms with a diligent regard for native costume, was early evidenced in the formation of the Napoleonic Mamelukes of the Guard.

The Mamelukes, like the Janissaries of Turkey, were originally slaves of various nationalities who gradually assumed ever-increasing power and finally turned the tables on there former Egyptian masters by ruling the whole country. A fine, soldierly body, they fought with great valour against the invading French in 1798, and their magnificent charge under Mourad Bey at the Pyramids so impressed Bonaparte that he resolved to form a regiment of these warriors for the service of the Republic.

They were later embodied in the Imperial Guard, serving in such diverse capitals as Paris, Vienna, Berlin, Madrid and Moscow, and distinguishing themselves particularly at Austerlitz.

In the Peninsula they were attached, at the strength of one squadron, to the *Chasseurs à Cheval de la Garde.* By that time (as in the Zouaves of a later period) recruiting was no longer limited to Orientals. While the famous Roustan, the Emperor's personal Mameluke, was certainly a Georgian, there were also such personalities as St-Denis, known as Ali, whose 'souvenirs' were published in 1927, and Ducel, whose photograph appears in Lachouque's 'Anatamy of Glory'.

POLISH LANCERS OF THE GUARD

This regiment was created by decree on March 2, 1807 under the name of *Chevaulegers Polonais de la Garde,* and was raised on April 16, of the same year at a strength of four squadrons of two companies each.

At first it was to have had white jackets and crimson overalls for full-dress occasions, but in view of the troops leaving Warsaw in their blue service dress (Fig 32) and staying but a short time in France before going to Spain, the dress uniform was never issued, except to the band.

The Regiment was first employed on police duties in Madrid, in May 1808, but at Medina de Rio Sels, on July 14 of the same year, it took part in the battle in which the French captured 18 guns and an important number of colours and muskets. On the same occasion one squadron alone dispersed the entire Spanish regiment of the Queen's Dragoons; and on another, the French trumpet-major, Blaise Desey, had his horse shot under him. Nothing remarkable in that, of course; but the next minute the gallant NCO re-appeared, mounted on a donkey, and declaring that it was not the mount that made the soldier, but the spirit of the rider!

When the Emjeror left Madrid in January 1809, the regiment was ordered back to Valladolid, and then to France as an escort for Napoleon. The Austrian Campaign was in preparation, which the Poles attended as a Guard Unit, returning to Chantilly at its conclusion. From there, 400 men were again sent to Spain on the 10th and 16th of December, 1809, and it was just before they crossed the Spanish border in February the following year that they were given lances, thus becoming *Chevaulegers-Lanciers.*

They took part as such in the battle of Fuentes de Onoro, but were kept in reserve; and the detachment finally returned to France, at a strength of 315 men to rejoin the bulk of the Regiment.

DRAGOONS

The green coat of the French Dragoons first appeared in the late 18th century and remained in wear until the latter part of Napoleon III's reign, when it was changed to blue.

At the beginning of the First Empire there were 30 regiments of this arm in existence, many being formed from amalgamations of units due for disbandment and others serving as a framework for the raising of new regiments. They were distinguished by a range of facing colours allocated on systematic rather than a traditional basis, so that the Peninsular regiments would have appeared as follows:

Regiment	Lapels and Turnbacks	Collar	Cuffs	Cuff-slash	Pockets
2nd	scarlet	scarlet	scarlet	scarlet	across
4th	scarlet	scarlet	scarlet	scarlet	vertical
6th	scarlet	scarlet	green	scarlet	vertical
8th	crimson	green	crimson	green	across
13th	pink	pink	pink	pink	across
15th	pink	pink	green	pink	across
16th	pink	pink	pink	pink	vertical
17th	pink	green	pink	green	vertical
18th	pink	pink	green	pink	vertical
19th	primrose	primrose	primrose	primrose	across
21st	primrose	primrose	green	primrose	across

DRAGOONS

LEFT: Pioneer of the 16th Dragoons wearing a bearskin cap, worn also by elite companies, and an officer of the 4th Dragoons. RIGHT: Corporal of Dragoons in the normal dress for line companies. The coatee was green, breeches white. Note how NCO chevrons were worn.

Regiment	Lapels and Turnbacks	Collar	Cuffs	Cuff-slash	Pockets
22nd	primrose	primrose	primrose	primrose	vertical
25th	aurore	aurore	aurore	aurore	across
26th	aurore	green	aurore	green	across
27th	aurore	aurore	green	aurore	across
28th	aurore	aurore	aurore	aurore	vertical

'Aurore'—a colour peculiar to France—is a rich golden yellow with a touch of salmon pink.

Elite companies and pioneers wore a bearskin cap and scarlet fringed epaulettes, attributes which, according to the Alsatian collections of paper soldiers, were also worn in white by the other ranks in the 2nd, 17th and 19th Regiments in the years 1807–8.

Officers as in most of the other arm were dressed as the rank-and-file, except in finer cloth, and their rank was shown by the silver epaulettes which corresponded with the white-metal buttons worn by all regiments. The 3rd Dragoons were withdrawn from Spain in 1811 to form the 2nd Lancers at Celle in the following year.

CHASSEURS A CHEVAL

As in most countries, the French light cavalry came into existence in the mid-18th century, but here at its inception, took the form of detachments attached to existing troops. They became regularly organised in 1757, and in 1776 they were embodied in various legions of volunteers. Later they were attached to the dragoon regiments at a strength of one squadron per regiment, and soon afterwards, in 1779, these squadrons were amalgamated to form 6 regiments of *Chasseurs à Cheval* each comprising four mounted squadrons and one foot battalion of four companies.

The number of regiments increased continually until, under the Empire, a total of 31 regiments appeared on the establishment. They were all clothed in green, with turnbacks and piping in the facing colour, which was also present—according to regiments on collar and/or cuffs. Thus, the regiments engaged in the Peninsula would be distinguished as follows:

10th, crimson collar and cuffs; 13th, orange collar and cuffs; 14th, green collar and orange cuffs; 15th, orange collar and green cuffs; 21st, aurore collar and green cuffs; 22nd, nasturtium collar and cuffs; 26th, green collar and red cuffs (Fig 33).

The remaining four regiments were rather special units, having been formed from other corps, some of them foreign. The 27th were none other than the *Chevaulégers d'Aremberg*, a Belgian regiment which, in 1809, wore a green hussar jacket with a red collar; the 28th, with maroon collar and cuffs, was originally the Toscan Dragoons; the 29th, with maroon cuffs, came from the 3rd Provisional Cavalry Regiment, and the 31st—the only chasseur regiment wearing a buff collar and cuffs—was formed from two provisional regiments of Polish cavalry. Indeed, the whole uniform was Polish in design, even to the czapka head-dress.

Hair was normally cut short in the modern fashion, but in the 15th and 26th queues were worn until 1813.

The head-dress was the standard bell-topped shako, with a plume in various combinations of dark green and red, and white-metal fittings to agree with the buttons on the coat.

Elite companies wore a black busby with a tall frontal plume and sometimes scarlet epaulettes; while trumpeters are to be found in all sorts of colourful costume, chiefly in reversed colours. For instance, a print exists showing a trumpeter of the 14th in an orange coat with green lapels, cuffs and shoulder-straps, as well as a black busby with a white plume and scarlet bag. He wears grey overalls with a double yellow band.

HUSSARS

Unlike their British counterparts, the first French Hussars were genuine Hungarian horsemen recruited in 1691 for Louis XIV by several officers deserting from the Imperial service. They undertook to provide a complete light cavalry regiment, fully mounted and equipped, from a number of troops who had followed them.

Further regiments were added later, including one raised in Turkey by Count Bercheny in 1719, and another at Strasbourg, by Count Esterhazy, in 1734. These truly Hungarian names were to become famous in the annals of the French Hussars and remained as regimental titles well into the First Empire.

We learn from Fortescue that the 1st, 2nd, 3rd, 22nd and 26th Hussars took part in the Peninsular War (at least in the second phase), although it is difficult to understand what is meant by the last two, since there were no more than twleve regiments in existence, numbered consecutively (Fig 34, 35, 36). It is likely, in fact, that there is confusion here with the 22nd and 26th *Chasseurs à Cheval,* who were certainly present; but on the other hand, the 12th Regiment is not mentioned, although it was raised in Spain in 1812, from three squadrons of the 9th, and clothed in a scarlet jacket, with light blue collar and cuffs, and light blue pelisse (with black fur) and breeches. All lacing was white, and the shako had a black plume tipped in lime yellow, and white-metal eagle plate and chin-scales.

LANCIERS DE BERG

The German territory of Berg, with its capital Düsseldorf, was ceded to Napoleon in 1806, who advanced it to the rank of a Grand Duchy under Joachim Murat. Two years later, however, the title of Grand Duke of Berg passed to Napoléon-Louis, a younger son of King Louis of Holland : in other words, to the Emperor's nephew and a brother of the future Napoleon III.

The army of this small state comprised cavalry, artillery and infantry dressed in dark green, blue and white respectively; but the cavalry consisted only of one regiment of light horse, raised in 1807. On December 17, 1809, however, the regiment became lancers and was posted to the Imperial Guard under the name of *Lanciers de Berg.* 'By that means', wrote Napoleon to his Minister for War, the Duke of Feltre, 'I shall have in my Guard two regiments of lancers : one of Polish Chevaulégers and the other of *'Chevaulégers de Berg'.*

The white uniform was no doubt used for full-dress occasions, because there is also evidence of a dark green order of dress, which was probably the former *chasseur* uniform, now doing duty as service dress. It is indeed possible that the white and crimson dress was simply the intended Polish uniforms taken out of store and issued to the Germans.

A print by Martinet, reproduced in Lachouque's *Anatomy of Glory,* shows white epaulettes on both shoulders, a somewhat unlikely disposition in view of the French lancer regulations which specified a shoulder-cord only on the aiguillette side. In this print the absence of a czapka-plate and waist-belt also seems a little suspect, but the white buttonhole loops which it shows may be more accurate than the Marbot version given here (Fig 37).

GENDARMES-CHEVAULEGERS or LANCIERS-GENDARMES

Also known as the *Gendarmes d'Espagne,* the Imperial Gendarmerie in Spain raised in December 1810, consisted of 20 squadrons, numbered consecutively Each squadron was divided into one company of *Lanciers-Gendarmes* (of 3 officers, 10 NCO's and 40 other ranks) and one company of dismounted Gendarmes numbering 2 officers, 10 NCO's and 110 other ranks.

In addition, a legion in Catalonia (numbered 6th in December, 1811) consisted of 6 squadrons, each one comprising two companies of dismounted gendarmes and one platoon of horse: in all, a total of 1,400 men of whom 162 were mounted. There was also a legion at Burgos, at a strength of 6 companies, each with 7 officers and 125 NCOs and other ranks.

After the French had evacuated Spain at the end of the war, the whole body of *Gendarmes d'Espagne* was assembled at Auch, in southern France, and later disbanded by virtue of the Decree of November 21, 1813. This was shortly before the opening of the campaign in France, and the disbanded gendarmes were therefore re-grouped into three mobile columns to act against deserters and such like. In Spain, however, their chief duty appears to have been to combat the *guerrilleros* who constantly harassed the French troops, and they are reputed to have been examples of good discipline.

Many different descriptions of the uniform exist, but all agree on a dark blue coat, though some give blue breeches and others buff. However, the uniform shown here (Fig 38) is based on the official regulations of 1812, although one cannot be certain that they were followed to the letter.

The lance-pennon was usually red-over-white and the horse-furniture consisted of a dark blue shabraque with a 3 inch white border and round valise of the same. A white grenade was set at 45° ; in the rear corners of the shabraque.

The officers somewhat unexpectedly, retained their mounted Gendarmerie uniform with the bicorne hat, and although no official mention is made of trumpeters, both the Alsatian collections and the Marckolsheim MS show figures in a red coat with blue facings, and blue breeches as in the rank-and-file.

FRENCH FOOT ARTILLERY (GUARD) 1808-11
Drum Major
HAT: White plume. Feathers: one light blue between two red. Gold ornaments. Tricolour cockade.
COAT, WAISTCOAT, BREECHES: Blue. Scarlet collar, lapels, turnbacks. Gold epaulettes, lace, stripes, buttons.
BELT: Scarlet. Gold ornaments.
GLOVES: Gold lace. STAFF: Silver fittings.

ARTILLERY

The true value of artillery was first appreciated by Louis XIV who, as early as 1668, organised it on a sound military basis when he assembled the rather loose formation of gunners and bombardiers attached to sundry garrisons throughout the kingdom and formed them into a permanent corps. The mobile aspect was recognised later, and the King raised the *Fusiliers du Roy* on February 4, 1671, as a body not only of fusiliers, but also of gunners, sappers, woodworkers and artificers.

On April 15, 1693, the corps took the name of *Régiment Royal de l'Artillerie* and formed the nucleus of an ever-expanding structure which, by the time of the Peninsular War, included Guard and Line branches, with Horse and Foot regiments in each.

The Horse Artillery of the Guard was dressed hussar-fashion, and all ranks except officers wore moustaches and clubbed hair, as well as the golden earings which were then authorised in the Guard. The uniform was a sober dark blue throughout, with pointed cuffs of scarlet, and all lacing, breeches-bands and Austrian knots were in the same colour. The pelisse, with black fur edging, followed the same pattern, and the busby-ornaments, with those of the blue shabraque, were scarlet likewise. All buttons were brass, and the horses were black.

The Foot branch wore the regulation artillery uniform, but with a bearskin cap, which in this case was fitted with a peak, and the scarlet epaulettes of a *corps d'élite.*

In the Line, the hussar dress was again present in the Horse branch, but here the busby was replaced by a bell-topped shako with scarlet ornaments and brass fittings. However, no pelisse was worn; hair was cut short, and earrings were not allowed.

As regards the Foot branch, the dark blue uniform with scarlet cuffs and piping was soon supplemented with various makeshift and unofficial garments, as dictated by the rigours of the Spanish winter. In this, of course, the Artillery was not alone, for the entire army was eventually reduced to these expedients; but in any event, regulations provided for an oilskin shako-cover for bad weather, as well as a long grey or dark blue greatcoat as a protection against the cold. (Fig 42)

INFANTRY OF THE GUARD

On May 3, 1808, the first four Fusilier battalions of the Guard arrived at Bayonne, but when they had reached Poitiers they had been divided into one regiment each of Fusiliers-Grenadiers and Fusiliers-Chasseurs. The famous Grenadiers and Chasseurs were also on their way, as well as the Sailors of the Guard, who in reality were more military than naval.

The Fusiliers were to the Grenadiers and Chasseurs what the battalion companies were to grenadier and light infantry companies in the Line. However, since they were differentiated as Fusilier-Grenadiers and Fusilier-Chasseurs, their uniform appears never to have been properly regulated, and to quote Rousselot (Plate 101). 'Popular works (on the subject), both ancient and modern, always consider the question of uniform as definitely settled matter directly a new unit was raised, whereas it was nothing of the sort, either in the Guard or in the Line.'

In this case, the uniform in both sections seems to have followed the regular pattern of the Guard, ie, collar in the same colour as the coat, and scarlet cuffs and turnbacks. The Fusiliers-Grenadiers' cuffs were cut square, with white 3-button slashes (Fig 39), while in the Chasseurs they were pointed (Fig 40). Another difference was that the Grenadiers' epaulettes were red with a white fringe, those of the Chasseurs were green with a scarlet fringe. But, of course, many variations are to be found, as well as many different versions of plumes.

The regiments of Grenadiers and Chasseurs, far better known, wore the traditional bearskin cap, with a brass plate and scarlet ornaments for the Grenadiers, and no plate but a scarlet-over-green plume for the Chasseurs. The Grenadiers' epaulettes were all-scarlet, and their cuffs were the same as the Fusiliers-Grenadiers', while in the Chasseurs these were respectively green (with scarlet crescent and fringe), and scarlet (pointed) piped in white. For the rest, both bodies wore the blue coat with white lapels and blue collar, and white waiscoat and breeches with either white or black gaiters.

It is unlikely, however, that the Guard took part in any major battles in the Peninsula, for the Emperor wrote to Berthier, 'The Guard is not part of the Army', and to King Joseph, 'I want my Guard to remain at rest, so as to be in a condition to move to another front in case of need'. He was, of course, contemplating another war in Austria.

SAILORS OF THE GUARD

It has never been quite clear whether these troops were sailors or marines. Their French designation of *Matelots* (or *Marins*) certainly means 'sailors', for the French for 'Marine' is *Infanterie de la Marine.* However, it cannot be denied that the corps could have had little, if any sea service.

The full dress uniform was dark blue throughout, with a hussar-type jacket laced in *aurore* and long trousers. The shako, with a brass eagle plate and

Tambour-major of the band of the Grenadiers of the Imperial Guard in his distinctive and decorative parade dress. Gauntlets, breeches, and plastron front of the coatee are all white, embellished with gold lace. The fringes at the ankles are red, the coatee blue, and facings and braid are red. The bicorne hat has extensive gold lace and red, white and blue plumes. Hair is powdered white and pigtailed (Pierre Althert print from author's collection).

scarlet plume, carried *aurore* ornaments, and the pointed cuffs were scarlet. In service dress, however, the shako was covered in black oilskin, while the jacket was replaced by a simple double breasted, all-blue garment. The *aurore* lacing was retained on collar and cuffs, as were the black cross-belts and brass shoulder-scales of the full dress. Buttons were brass throughout (Fig 59).

These troops were most unfortunate in the Peninsula. Their main battle was at Bayléy, on July 19, 1808, in which a whole French army was surrounded and forced to surrender. For the Sailors, the position was quite hopeless, for in the words of their Commanding Officer, Captain Grivel, 'We were in a mouse-trap'.

INFANTRY OF THE LINE

At the proclamation of the Empire, the Infantry of the Line's uniform remained as it was, and in fact foot soldiers of 1805 looked very much like those of 1793, even to the bicorne hat. That article, however, prone as it was to lose its shape in bad weather, and inadequate to protect the head from sabre-cuts, was replaced in 1807 by the bell-topped shako which one commonly, associates with Napoleonic infantry. The fittings were brass and the plate could be in the shape of an Imperial Eagle or a diamond stamped in relief with either a plain numeral or the Eagle. In full dress, white cords and a ball-tuft were worn. (Fig 41).

Note: 30th Line Regiment is used to illustrate Line Regiment dress of the Peninsular War period, though this particular regiment is not recorded as having taken part in the campaign.

FRENCH 30th LINE REGIMENT 1807-13
Light Company, 1809
SHAKO: Yellow-over-green plume. Green cords. Yellow band. Brass fittings. WAISTCOAT, BREECHES: White
COAT: Blue. Yellow collar. Green epaulettes (yellow crescent). Scarlet cuffs, slashes, piping. White lapels and turnbacks. Brass buttons.
EQUIPMENT: Fawn pack and greatcoat
SWORD: Brass fittings. Green knot
(regulation dress, after Rousselot)

In the same year, for reasons of economy, the blue coat was to be replaced by a white one, with various facing colours appearing on collars, lapels, cuffs, etc, according to a system whereby all regiments would be indicated differently. But the many disadvantages of a white uniform soon became apparent, and as early as January 28 1807, the Emperor wrote, 'I am very dissatisfied with the white coats. Give orders for issues of blue cloth'. Thus, very few units received the white coats, although some were seen in Spain a few years later, since they were to remain in use until worn out.

The flank companies were distinguished from the others in characteristic manner. The grenadiers wore black bearskin caps with brass plates, scarlet plumes and white cords, or a regulation shako with a tall scarlet plume and cords of the same colour. The voltigeurs had yellow collars, green cords on the shako, and plumes and epaulettes in various combinations of green and yellow. All flank companies were armed with a short sword, as well as a bayonet, and were entitled to wear moustaches. Further, the grenadiers wore scarlet grenades on their turnbacks, and the voltigeurs yellow bugle-horns; they also carried the same attributes in brass on their pouch-flaps .Grenadiers had scarlet sword-knots and voltigeurs green; and the sword had a further use in providing a rigid support for carrying the tall plume when not in wear. It was simply placed in a sheath and tied to the scabbard.

The officers wore basically the same dress, their rank being shown by gold epaulettes, as follows: Colonel, two with bullion fringe; Major, the same, but with silver straps; Battalion Commander, as Colonel ,but no fringe on right shoulder; Captain, the same, but fringe of gold twist; Adjutant, as Captain, but on reverse shoulders; Lieutenant, as Captain, but scarlet line along centre of straps; Sous-Lieutenant, the same, but two lines.

At this period, drummers and musicians wore all manner of colourful costume,

FRENCH 30th LINE REGIMENT

Drummer, 1809-10

SHAKO: Red plume and band. White cords. Brass fittings.
COAT: Red. Blue collar, wings, lapels, cuffs and slashes, turnbacks. Yellow lace. Brass buttons.
WAISTCOAT, BREECHES, APRON, BELT: White. Brass plate. EQUIPMENT: Fawn pack and greatcoat.
SWORD: Brass fittings. Red knot.
DRUM: Brass. Blue hoops
(after Tanconville, "Garn. d'Alsace..")

FRENCH 30th LINE REGIMENT 1807-13

Drum Major, 1809-10

BUSBY: Brass grenade. Red bag and tassel.
COAT: Red. Blue collar, cuffs and slashes, lapels, wings, stripes, turnbacks. Gold lace, epaulettes, buttons.
WAISTCOAT, BREECHES, GAITERS, BELT: White. Brass plate.
SWORD: Brass fittings. Red knot.
STAFF: Brass fittings. Tricolour cords.
(after Tanconville, "Garn. d'Alsace..")

in many cases designed or approved by the commanding officers personally. The tall figure of the drum major was particularly resplendent in most regiments, although the rank was no more than sergeant-major. Of these, the drum major of the 8th Regiment, in 1808, wore a dark blue coat with crimson collar, cuffs, and lapels, and a profusion of gold lace, while his bicorne hat was also laced in gold and carried a monumental plume between four ostrich feathers—all these in white. In the 45th, at the same period, he wore the same collar and lace, but light blue facings, and for head-dress a black busby with a light blue bag and in front a mid-blue plume between red ostrich feathers. In boht cases waistcoat and breeches were white, and buff-topped boots were worn in the 8th, while gold-laced Hessians appeared in the 45th.

In the 96th, a voltigeur drummer of 1809-10, was clothed in the regulation blue coat with yellow collar and green epaulettes, but with crimson lapels and cuffs, while the shako, with its green cords, carried a scarlet-over-yellow plume rising from a green ball-tuft.

The regimental Colours were not yet designed in the three vertical bands of blue, white and red. The staff, of course, carried the Eagle (which was the main emblem) and the pattern on the silk was basically a large white diamond enclosed in four triangles of blue, red, red and blue. The wording, in gold lettering on the white, read, 'L'EMPEREUR / DES FRANCAIS / AU.... REGIMENT / D'INFANTERIE / DE LIGNE, while each triangle bore the regiment's numeral in an elaborate laurel wreath, in gold likewise. There was a straight border of gold laurel leaves separating the coloured triangles from the white, and a gold fringe ornamented the three outer edges.

So far as can be ascertained, the following line infantry regiments participated in the Peninsular War: 1-8, 10, 12, 14, 15, 16, 22, 24, 26, 27, 28, 31, 32, 34,

36, 37, 39, 40, 43, 44, 45, 47, 50, 51, 54, 55, 56, 57, 58, 59, 62, 63, 64, 66, 69, 70, 75, 76, 77, 82, 86, 88, 93, 94, 95, 96, 100, 101, 103, 114, 116, 117, 118, 119, 120, 121 and 122.

LIGHT INFANTRY

This branch was not organised on a regular basis until late in the 18th century, but a number of light units had previously existed as independant bodies, sometimes even as composite formations—such as the *Chasseurs de Fischer*.—of light cavalry and infantry. The association with cavalry, however, remained in operation for some years, for on May 8, 1784, the foot troops were amalgamated in 6 battalions of 4 companies each and attached to 6 existing regiments of *Chasseurs à Cheval.*

At the beginning of the Empire there were 26 light regiments in existence, but by the time of the First Abdication the number had risen to 35, and in the Peninsula, the following are recorded as having taken part: 1, 2, 3, 4, 5, 9, 12, 15, 16, 17, 18, 21, 25, 27, 28 31 and 32. They were organised in battalions and companies, on the same pattern as the Line, and indeed their function was no different either, so that the only distinction between the two arms was one of designation and appearance.

As in the Line, there were grenadier, battalion and light companies, but here they were called carabiniers, chasseurs, and voltigeurs respectively. The carabiniers wore a bearskin cap, scarlet epaulettes and scarlet grenades on the turnbacks, but for the remainder the standard shako and white bugle-horns were the rule. Scarlet collars and green epaulettes or blue shoulder-straps distinguished the chasseurs, while the voltigeurs wore yellow collars, and epaulettes in which green, yellow and sometimes scarlet were present in

16th LIGHT INFANTRY

Voltigeur *1807–10* *Cornettist*

15th LIGHT INFANTRY

Pioneer. (White apron and gloves, plus busby—remainder of uniform generally as other ranks) 1809.

Musician. (Note extra braid on tunic and breeches and light coloured shako) 1809.

15th LIGHT INFANTRY

Cantiniere (left) (female attendant) and Carabinier, showing bearskin hat worn by carabinier company 1809.

17th LIGHT REGIMENT
Warrant Officer (note braided shako and chevrons on sleeve) 1805–10.

27th LIGHT REGIMENT
Chasseur, showing plain blue shoulder straps 1807–09.

various combinations. There are also instances of these light companies wearing busbies.

The light infantry was heavily engaged throught the Peninsular Campaign, and many eye-witness accounts have survived; but a recently-discovered diary, kept by Corporal Colomb of the 17th, makes very interesting reading. It was edited by Donald D. Howard and published in the *Journal of the Society for Army Historical Research* (Vol XLVI, No 185).

SWISS REGIMENTS

When a Swiss protests indignantly that his compatriots in foreign service were not mercenaries, but allies, he is perfectly right. Admittedly, Swiss mercenaries were certainly present in many armies of the Renaissance period, but from the 18th century onwards recruiting was organised on a state to state and properly supervised basis. The Swiss regiments were fully-operational units which Switzerland lent to other countries, and the cantons had a perfect right to withdraw their troops should they so desire.

So far as France was concerned, even before the proclamation of the Empire, a Treaty of Alliance had been signed at Fribourg between that country and Switzerland on September 27, 1803. France agreed to defend Switzerland, while Switzerland would supply 16,000 troops divided into four regiments, plus four companies of Artillery. Men between the ages of 18 and 40 were eligible and would serve for four years, in Europe only. Their pay was fixed at 1.20 francs for fusiliers and 1.25 francs for grenadiers.

Thus, during the First Empire, four regiments of Swiss infantry were on the strength of the French army, all clothed in the red coat traditional to these

SWISS REGTS. IN FRENCH SERVICE 1805-15
Private, 1st Rgt. 1805-6

SHAKO: Red ball-tuft; white cords; brass plate; tricolour cockade.
COAT: Red; yellow collar, lapels, cuffs; white turnbacks; blue piping. Brass buttons.
WAISTCOAT, BREECHES, BELTS: White.
(after Lienhart & Humbert: "L'Armée Francaise")

SWISS REGTS. IN FRENCH SERVICE 1805-15
Field Officer, 2nd Rgt. 1814-5

HAT: Tricolour cockade; gold loop and bosses.
COAT: Red; blue collar, lapels, cuffs, cuff-slash, turnbacks. Gold epaulettes. Gilt buttons.
WAISTCOAT, BREECHES, GLOVES: White.
SWORD: Black and gilt; gold knot.
(after de Vallière: "Honneur et Fidélité")

Note: Not all the Swiss regiments shown here served in the Peninsular.

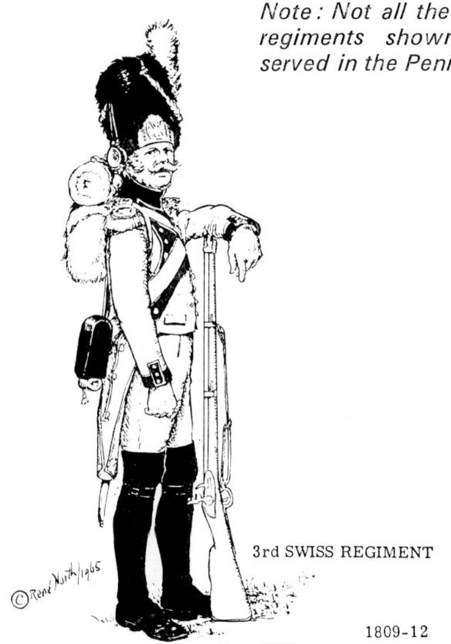

3rd SWISS REGIMENT 1809-12
Grenadier, 1809

BEARSKIN: Scarlet plume. White cords. Tricolour cockade. Brass plate.
COAT: Red. White epaulettes, piping, turnbacks (red grenades). Brass buttons.
WAISTCOAT, BREECHES, BELTS: White.
EQUIPMENT: Fawn pack. Grey coat. Red cap (white tassel) under pouch. (after Carl Collection, Strasbourg)

3rd SWISS REGIMENT 1809-12
Fusilier, 1809

SHAKO: Orange ball. Tricolour cockade. White cords. Brass fittings.
COAT: Red. White piping and turnbacks. Brass buttons.
WAISTCOAT, BREECHES, BELT: White.
(after Carl Collection, Strasbourg)

(after Carl Collection)

3rd SWISS REGIMENT 1809-12
Drummer, 1809

BEARSKIN: Scarlet plume. White cords. Tricolour cockade. Brass plate.
COAT: Scarlet. Blue collar, lapels, cuffs (scarlet slash, piped white). Gold lace and buttons.
EPAULETTES, WAISTCOAT, BREECHES, BELTS: White. Brass fittings. DRUM: Brass. Blue hoops.

SWISS REGTS. IN FRENCH SERVICE 1805-15
Private, 4th Rgt. 1812

SHAKO: Red ball-tuft; brass eagle and scales; tricolour cockade.
COAT: Red, sky-blue collar, lapels, cuffs, turnbacks; blue piping. Brass buttons.
BREECHES, BELTS: White.
(after de Vallière: "Honneur et Fidélité")

BERTHIER'S NEUCHATEL BATTALION 1810-12

Voltigeur, 1810

SHAKO: Green plume and cords; tricolour cockade; brass fittings.
COAT: Yellow; scarlet collar (piped yellow), lapels, cuffs, slashes, turnbacks; silver buttons; green epaulettes edged yellow.
TROUSERS, GAITERS, BELTS: White.
SWORD: Brass fittings; green knot.
(after copy contemp. w/colour, Neuchâtel Museum)

BERTHIER'S NEUCHATEL BATTALION 1810-12
Private, 1812

SHAKO: White ball-tuft; tricolour cockade; brass fittings.
COAT: Yellow; scarlet collar (piped yellow), lapels, cuffs, slashes, turnbacks; silver buttons.
EPAULETTES, BELTS, BREECHES: White.
(after copy contemp. w/colour, Neuchâtel Museum)

BERTHIER'S NEUCHATEL BATTALION 1810-12

Grenadier Officer, 1810

CAP: Scarlet plume; silver cords and flounders.
COAT: Yellow; scarlet collar (piped yellow), cuffs, lapels, turnbacks; silver epaulettes (red lines), gorget (gilt eagle), buttons.
BELT, BREECHES: White; silver plate; gilt badge.
SWORD: Gilt fittings; gold and red knot.
(after portrait, Colombier Museum)

BERTHIER'S NEUCHATEL BATTALION 1810-12

Gunner, 1812

SHAKO: Scarlet tuft and rim; brass fittings; tricolour cockade.
COAT, BREECHES: Blue; yellow collar and cuffs (piped red); yellow piping; scarlet epaulettes and turnbacks; silver buttons.
BELTS: White.
SWORD: Brass fittings; scarlet knot.
(after copy contemp. w/colour, Neuchâtel Museum)

troops. They were distinguished by facing colours on the collar, lapels and cuffs as follows: 1st Regiment, yellow; 2nd, dark blue; 3rd, black, and 4th, light blue.

But the great disadvantage, and indeed tragedy, of the system was that Swiss nationals could find themselves on opposing sides in war, a case in point being the battle of Baylen, in Spain, on July 19, 1808. Christen's battalion of the red-coated 5th Swiss Regiment found itself confronted by the 'Old-Reding' Regiment of *Suizos azulos* ('Blue Swiss') in the Spanish service. Greetings were exchanged, fraternisation took place—then suddenly, for some unexplained reason, a minor quarrel broke out and in no time the Swiss of both sides were fighting fiercely.

Understandably, this incident led to a re-assessment of the troops' conditions of service, and in future no Swiss would find himself in a position where he could kill, or be killed by a compatriot.

It is not quite clear whether this provision applied equally to the Neuchâtel and Valais battalions raised for the Imperial service, because their situation was somewhat different. Neuchâtel, hitherto under the tutelage of the King of Prussia, was ceded to France in 1806 and declared a principality under Marshal Berthier, who assumed the title of Alexander, Prince of Neuchâtel. On May 11, 1807, an Imperial Decree announced the formation of a Neuchâtel Battalion, with a company of artillery, engineers and transport. The battalion was to be clothed in yellow (hence its nickname of *Les Canaris*) while the ancillary companies were to be in dark blue. They took part in the battle of Wagram in 1809, and were in Spain for the rest of the Peninsular Campaign, mostly employed in convoy duties and anti-guerilla activities. They left Valladolid in early February 1812, arriving at Bayonne on March 10—in time, incidentally, for the disastrous Russian Campaign.

The Valais, in southern Switzerland, was an independent republic when it concluded an arrangement with France just before the proclamation of the First Empire. This provided for the raising of an infantry battalion with its depot at Turin for service in the French forces (Fig 43). Little is known of the regiment's activities in Spain, but it was probably employed on escort duties. However after the Valais became part of France as Dept. 7 : Simplon, the battalion was disbanded at Wesel on November 12, 1810 and absorbed into the 11th Light Infantry Regiment.

THE HANOVERIAN LEGION

In June 1803, after the rupture of the Peace of Amiens, France occupied the Kingdom of Hanover. Baron von Decken was then successfully conducting a more or less clandestine recruiting campaign for the King's German Legion in Great Britain; a state of affairs which Napoleon immediately countered by charging General Mortier with the raising of a Hanoverian Legion for the French service. The corps was finally approved on April 13, 1804, in the form of a regiment of light infantry and one of mounted chasseurs.

The infantry, at a strength of 703 men, formed part of General Loison's 3rd Division in the 1st Observation Corps of the Gironde (Army of Portugal) and was brigaded, under Brigadier General Simon, with the 26th Light Infantry and the Légion du Midi.

It was in that formation that it participated in the battle of Busaco, on September 27, 1810, fighting successfully against the Rifle Brigade and the 1st and 3rd Caçadores until the 43rd and 52nd Light Infantry came to their rescue and repulsed the French.

Meanwhile, the 1st Battalion of the Regiment of Westphalia had been drafted to the Hanoverian Legion on September 30, 1809; but on August 9, 1811, the whole unit was disbanded. The infantry was distributed among the 127th, 128th and 129th Line Regiments, as well as in the 3rd Berg Regiment and the 2nd and 4th Foreign (Isembourg and Prussian respectively). The cavalry went either to the 1st Hussars or the 9th Lancers.

The Regiment, with its red coat and dark blue facings, could easily have been mistaken for the 2nd Swiss, since the white-metal badges of the Hanoverians were not always easy to distinguish. (Fig 49). A letter from Mortier, dated April 9, 1804, ordered officers to obtain silver epaulettes and states with delightful candour that NCOs would be armed with short swords 'found in the country'.

In the cavalry branch, according to the same source, several versions of dress were in existence, but cavalry appear to have worn a red coat with yellow facings, as well as the regulation shako. Officers are shown in a black busby with a white and red plume and gold epaulettes, while trumpeters are given a yellow coat with red lacing around the collar and red cuff-slashes piped green. They wear a black busby with a red-over-white plume on the left and a red busby-bag piped white. (Fig 48)

POLISH ARTILLERY AND INFANTRY

After the Treaty of Tilsitt in 1807, the Polish Artillery was brought up to a strength of 3 battalions (one in each of the three infantry divisions) under the command of General Axamitowski.

Each battalion consisted of 3 companies of foot artillery (6 guns each), 1 company of sappers and 1 transport company.

In July 1808, a company of the 3rd Battalion was selected to accompany the three Polish Foot Regiments detailed for the Peninsula; and at the end of

POLISH FOOT ARTILLERY 1810-5
Gunner

SHAKO: Red plume and cords; brass fittings.
JACKET, TROUSERS: Dark green; red epaulettes and piping; brass buttons.
PACK: Fawn; grey roll.
EQUIPMENT: Brass fittings; red sword-knot; brass grenades.
(after Malibran & Chelminski)

POLISH FOOT ARTILLERY 1810-5
Captain

HAT: White cockade; gold ornaments.
COAT: Dark green; gold epaulettes and buttons; red piping.
WAISTCOAT, BREECHES: White
SWORD: Gold knot and fittings.
(after Malibran & Chelminski)

POLISH FOOT ARTILLERY 1810-5
Bombardier (summer dress)

SHAKO: Red plume and cords; brass fittings.
JACKET: Dark green; red epaulettes and piping; brass buttons; yellow stripes.
BELT, TROUSERS, GAITERS: White
SCABBARD: Brass tip. (after Malibran & Chelminski)

POLISH INFANTRY 1810-14
5th Regiment. Grenadier Officer

CAP: Silver cords and eagle; brass plate; red plume.
COAT: Blue; white lapels; red piping and turnbacks; gold epaulettes and buttons.
WAISTCOAT, BREECHES, GLOVES: White.
BOOTS: Gold ornaments. SWORD: Gilt fittings.
(after Malibran and Chelminski)

POLISH HORSE ARTILLERY 1808-14
Officer, 1808
CZAPKA: Red plume and ball-tuft. Gold cords and fittings.
KURTKA: Dark green. Red piping. Gold epaulettes, buttons, belts. OVERALLS: Dark green. Red piping.
HORSE-FURNITURE: Dark green. Red piping and ornaments. (after Haykowski and regulations)

POLISH HORSE ARTILLERY 1808-14
Gunner, 1810
BUSBY: Red ornaments. Brass chin-scales.
UNIFORM: Dark green. Red piping. White belts. Brass buttons. Yellow grenades.
EPAULETTES: Brass scales. Red fringe
HORSE-FURNITURE: Dark green. Red border and piping. Yellow grenades.
(after Dress Regulations)

1809, the whole of the Foot Artillery was organised as one Regiment under Colonel Gorski. At this date the strength of the Foot and Horse Artillery amounted to a total of 2,620 men, but the Horse branch does not appear to have been employed in Spain.

In the meantime, early in 1808, Napoleon had persuaded Poland to join the Confederation of the Rhine and thereby had no difficulty in demanding from that country a contingent of troops for the invasion of Spain which he was then contemplating. These consisted of the 4th, 7th and 9th Infantry Regiments (i.e., one from each division) plus the Chevaulégers of the Guard and the Vistula Legion, although the last two units were really part of the French Army. These troops, with the exception of the Chevaulégers already in Spain, arrived at Bayonne towards the middle of the summer of 1808 and were posted to the 4th Army Corps under Marshal Lefebevre (Figs 44 and 45).

The army, under Marshal Soult crossed the Pyrenees at the end of October and on November 10, defeated a corps of 12,000 Spaniards.

Napoleon soon followed, but on January 2, 1809, news reached him of Austria's rapprochement with Great Britain. He therefore decided—as on several other notable occasions—that his presence was needed in France, and therefore entrusted his army to Marshal Soult, who continued his persuit of the British to Corunna, where they embarked on 17th and 18th of the same month.

The three infantry regiments distinguished themselves at Talavera on July 28, 1811, and at Almonacid on August 10, but after the battle of Sagonte (October 25, 1811) nothing more is heard of the Poles. Meanwhile, on October 11, of the same year, several British transports arrived at the small fortress of Fuengirola, on the coast between Malaga and Marbello, to disembark the 82nd and 89th Foot, with the Toledo Regiment of Spanish

Note: Polish Horse Artillery, shown left, are included even though they do not appear to have served in the Peninsular campaigns.

POLISH INFANTRY 1810-14
3rd Division. Voltigeur
SHAKO: Yellow cords; yellow-over-green plume; brass plate.
JACKET: Blue; white collar, plastron, cuffs; brass buttons; green epaulettes.
TROUSERS: Blue. BELTS: White.
SWORD: Brass fittings; (probably) green knot.
(regulation dress)

infantry (Fig 26) under General Lord Blayney. They were opposed by a minute force of 150 men of the 4th Polish Regiment, who though greatly outnumbered, managed to capture 50 officers and 140 men, including Lord Blayney himself.

THE VISTULA LEGION

In 1807 an Italo-Polish Legion was formed on the lines of the units raised in Italy some 10 years earlier, and on November 11, of the same year it was posted to the Westphalian Army until March 20, 1808. It was then taken on the strength of the French forces under the title of *Légion de la Vistule* and at this stage consisted of three infantry regiments and one of lancers.

The Vistula Legion fought with consistent steadiness in the Peninsula, taking part in both sieges of Saragossa. Indeed, in the second, which lasted from December 1808 to February 20, 1809, it lost as many as 1,390 men : almost a third of its total strength.

After the battle of Wagram (July 5-6, 1809) a large number of Austrian prisoners of Polish nationality were formed into a second Legion of three regiments. However, a full complement was never reached, and on February 18, 1810, the new Legion was amalgamated with the First as its 4th Regiment at a strength of some 2,000 men.

But casualties were heavy. The Poles, in fact, suffered such severe losses in the Peninsula that on June 18, 1813, the four regiments were amalgamated to form the *Régiment de la Vistule.* It was disbanded in 1814 but some elements remained at Rheims and were drafted into the 3rd Foreign (Irish) Regiment on the Emperor's return from Elba.

As for the Lancers, there was originally only one regiment in the Legion, but in early February 1811 a second was added. However, on June 18, of the same year both regiments were incorporated into the French army as the 7th and 8th Lancers. They also formed the nucleus of a new regiment, numbered 9th, and all three continued to wear the Polish dress instead of the green uniform and brass helmets of the French—in other words, a black czapka with a plume of the same colour, a dark blue jacket and overalls, with a primrose collar, lapels, cuffs (pointed) and overall-bands (double). Authorities disagree as to the colour of the epaulettes: either white or primrose; but the

VISTULA LEGION INFANTRY

Officer *1809–12* *Private*

VISTULA LEGION CAVALRY

POLISH CAVALRY 1807-15
Corporal, 9th Lancers

CAP: Brass fittings; silver eagle; white cords.
KURTKA: Blue; red collar and cuffs; brass buttons and epaulettes (white fringe); yellow chevrons piped red.
PIPING, BELTS: White (brass plate).
OVERALLS: Blue; red bands. SHEEPSKIN: White; red edging.
PENNON: Red over white. SWORD: Steel; white knot.
(from Dembinski Collection)

lance pennon was crimson-over-white. White gauntlets were worn, and the girdle was white, with three blue stripes.

THE BADEN CONTINGENT

In July 1808 Baden was required to supply one regiment of infantry and a battery of artillery for the Peninsula Campaign. Accordingly, on August 24, the contingent crossed the Rhine at Kehl, and the Spanish frontier on October 13.

The territory, formerly a margravate but then a grand-duchy, became part of the Confederation of the Rhine on July 12, 1806, with an army of two-cavalry regiments, some horse and foot artillery, four infantry regiments and one battalion of light infantry, plus of course the usual ancillary services.

The infantry regiment detailed for Spain was the 4th, and in addition to the artillery, a detachment of the transport corps was also present: a total of over 1,900 men, 169 horses and 31 vehicles. When the contigent reached Bayonne, it was posted to the German Division, of which, with the 2nd Nassau Regiment, it formed the 1st Brigade, under Colonel von Porbeck.

It saw considerable fighting: Medellin, Talavera, Almonacid and Ocana being its principal engagements. Indeed, after the British 23rd Light Dragoons had been cut up at Talavera, the band of the Baden regiment 'rescued' the ownerless helmets littering the ground, and for the remainder of the campaign appeared on every occasion in British headgear.

A contemporary print in colour shows these troops in a mountainous landscape evidently meant to be Spain. The infantry figures are dressed in uniforms of distinctly French appearance (Fig 52), which also applies to the transport section (Fig 54). On the other hand, a gunner in one corner (Fig 51), and an officer and NCO in another, are clothed in the typical Baden uniform.

In 1813 the regiment took part in the battles of Vittoria and the Bidassoa, but since the Nassau and Frankfurt contingents had deserted to the British, the Baden troops were brought to the rear. They were later disarmed, and in 1814 returned to their own country, mourning Colonel von Porbeck, who had been killed at Talavera.

NASSAU INFANTRY AND CAVALRY

Up to 1803 the Nassau troops consisted of no more than one regiment of infantry (Nassau-Weilburg), but in 1809 a second regiment was formed from two further Weilburg battalions. Both units wore the same uniform (Fig 47) and formed part of the 1st Brigade of the German Division in Spain.

Their record does not appear to be particularly praiseworthy, because on December 10, 1813, the 2nd Nassau Regiment went over to the British by order of the Commanding Officer, Colonel von Kruse—who reappears, incidentally, promoted to the rank of Brigadier-General, in charge of the independent Nassau Brigade at Waterloo. Consequently, the French authorities decided to act firmly, and on December 26, of the same year disarmed the 1st Regiment at Barcelona and sent it to Normandy. The prodecure was not universally welcome, for we find that a Voltigeur of that regiment insisted on being transferred to the French 18th Light Infantry. 'I was wounded three times in Catalonia', he explained, 'fighting alongside the French soldiers. I received a decoration, and I plead to be allowed to end my days with them.'

On the other hand, the 2nd Nassauers certainly earned two battle-honours: Mesas de Ibor and Medellin, and it is interesting to note that 85 years later the German Emperor confirmed those honours to their successors, the 2nd Nassau Infantry Regiment No. 88 in the Prussian Army.

As for the cavalry, here again the record appears disappointing. There was only one regiment in existence, in the form of a unit of light horse raised in 1805 by Colonel von Bismarck. The members were mostly wealthy volunteers—a deposit of 350 florins was required—and they were divided into two squadrons of 125 men each, plus a depot company of 72 men (Fig 46).

They went to Spain in 1808, but in view of the unreliability of their compatriots, they were disarmed at Gerona and Figuieré on December 26, 1813, at the same time as the infantry. They were then sent to Normandy with the others, where they stayed until the fall of the Empire in the following year.

Apart from that, mention should be made of the drill, which was first carried out according to Austrian regulations. Words of command were of course given in German, but later, when the French drill was adopted, the orders given in that language were apt to be misunderstood—perhaps intentionally!

The first headdress of this regiment was the characteristic black leather helmet and crest of the German troops, but this was later abandoned in favour of the busby shown in Fig 41.

FRANKFORT am MAIN INFANTRY

On July 18, 1806 the City of Frankfort was ordered, as a member of the Confederation of the Rhine, to provide a contingent of 968 troops to the French Empire. The quota was later raised to 1,500 men, distributed in one infantry regiment, one light infantry regiment and one squadron of Hussars.

Of the Hussars, nothing is known, but it is on record that the white Austrian-type clothing of the Line regiment—with its bicorne hat—was replaced, after the battle of Medellin, on May 20, 1809 by a blue uniform of French design (Fig 58). It was no doubt in that dress that the Frankfort Regiment campaigned for the rest of the Peninsular War, because the original clothing had become so worn that when the Franforters were ordered to bury the dead after Medellin, they appropriated the brown greatcoats of the dead Spaniards and had them made into trousers.

Blue or white trousers were issued as well; and the usual distinctions of the French flank companies were also to be seen.

The Light Infantry wore an all-green uniform with white-metal buttons, except for the waistcoat, which was yellow. The shako was green, and carried a tall black plume and cords in mixed red and white. The belts were black leather.

By 1813, however, the German troop were being demoralised and on December 10, the Frankfort contingent went over to the British side, on the same day as the Nassau troops.

WESTPHALIAN CONTINGENT

The Kingdom of Westphalia, under King Jerome Napoleon—another of the Bonaparte brothers—entered the Confederation of the Rhine on November 15, 1807 and thereby committed itself to supplying a large number of troops to the Emperor of the French.

King Jerome's army, consisting of all arms, was clothed in a distinctly French style. Indeed, the whole accent was French, for even the design of the Colours was modelled on the French pattern, some even displaying the Imperial Eagle; and while the inscriptions were eventually changed to German, they certainly appeared in French at the outset.

In 1808 the army comprised a Garde du Corps Regiment (Fig 60) and Chevaulégers of the Guard; two regiments each of Cuirassiers and Hussars, and one of Chevaulégers; while the infantry consisted of two Guard regiments (one of Grenadiers and another of Jagers), eight Line regiments, and light infantry. In addition, of course, there were the usual artillery and ancillary troops.

It is a little difficult to ascertain with precision which of these actually fought in the Peninsula, but we do know for a fact that the Westphalian *Chevaulégers-Lanciers* served under Suchet in 1813 (Fig 50), presumably armed with the lances which were authorised in 1811. A second regiment was to have been raised in October 1812, but the project fell through.

The Infantry of the Line, the most likely to have provided the bulk of the contingent, was in white, with facings colours on collar, lapels, cuffs and piping. But about 1810, the arrangement was altered to blue lapels for all regiments with the numeral appearing in white on the turnbacks. However, what part, if any they took in the fighting has so far eluded the writer.

ITALIAN NEAPOLITAN CONTINGENTS

Sir John Fortescue, in his *History of the British Army* (Vol IX, Appendices IV and V), states that an Italian Brigade was present at the battle of the Pyrenees on July 16, 1813. Unfortunately, he does not say how it was composed, nor what part it took in the fighting; and Suchet's Memoirs are no more informative, although they mention Neapolitan troops, without unfortunately, naming the units.

On the other hand, the *Dragons Napoléon* certainly appear under the year 1811: ie, Vice-King Eugene's of Italy's 2nd Dragoon Regiment. This regiment was in Treilhard's division in 1811. (The 1st was named 'The Queen's', and wore pink facings).

ITALIAN 2nd DRAGOON REGIMENT

Trooper *1812* *Drummer*

No doubt the Italian Brigade was formed from infantry regiments, and in that case the troops would be wearing white jackets and breeches, with black gaiters and shakos of French design. The facing colours, on collar, lapels, cuffs and turnbacks varied according to regiments, in sundry combinations of scarlet, and very dark green. There were seven such regiments in existence, but it is not known which were part of the brigade in Spain.

The Neapolitan infantry was clothed in white, with facing colours on collar, lapels, cuffs and turnbacks, but here every regiment had its own particular colour.

SPANISH CAVALRY

The well-nigh impossible task of listing the various Spanish units which took part in the war is made even more difficult by the fact that Spain was first on one side, then on the other, and in fact, at times, seems almost to have achieved the Gilbertian situation of being on both sides at once.

It is known, however, that the Queen's Dragoons (Fig 56) were present at the battle of Medina del Rio Seco on July 14, 1808, where they were beaten by a squadron of Polish Lancers of the Imperial Guard. There were eight dragoon regiments in existence at this date, all dressed in yellow but distinguished by different facing colours.

The only lancer regiment mentioned by Fortescue is that of la Mancha, a two-squadron regiment of which little seems to be known. However, the *Bibliothéque Nationale* in Paris has a print by Valmont showing a soldier of that regiment (Fig 57). The lance-pennon is in the form of a Spanish flag, but with an extra band of yellow at the upper and lower edges, while the shabraque is a green, round-cornered affair, with a green round valise edged in yellow. The shabraque carries a 3 inch yellow border, with a yellow grenade in front and a crowned circular device at the back. It is further ornamented with green dog's-teeth with a narrow yellow edging.

Both regiments of *Cazadores à Caballo* took part in the battle of the Pyrenees on July 16, 1813. They were the regular light horse regiments of Olivenza and *Voluntarios de España* dressed in green (Fig 55). A red plume and white lacing were worn in both regiments, but while the facings were red in the 1st Regiment, they were light blue in the second. The collar-badge was the traditional crossed sword and palm of the Spanish cavalry; and the horse-furniture consisted of a green shabraque, holster-caps and rectangular valise, all edged with a broad white border.

Napier cites several cavalry regiments present at the battle of Albuhera on May 16, 1811, but it has not been possible to identify all of them. However, the Queen's and the Bourbon Regiments were there, in blue coats and light blue collar, lapels and cuffs for the former, and scarlet for the latter; as well as the 'Algarve' Regiment, with yellow facings. The head-dress was a white-laced bicorne with a red bow, and the breeches were white.

SPANISH INFANTRY

In 1806 the Spanish Infantry of the Line went into a white uniform with a bicorne hat and black under-knee gaiters. There were 35 of these units, all distinguished by various colours of collar, cuffs, lapels and brass or silver buttons. In addition, four foreign regiments were clothed in light blue.

King Joseph's Guard is mentioned by Fortescue under the date of 1809. This was probably the Grenadier Regiment, which was copied in every respect on the French model, except for buff breeches and perhaps the inscription on the buttons (Fig 54). A print by Dighton in the Royal Gallery at Windsor shows soldier of the Toledo Regiment which was brigaded with the British 82nd and 89th Foot under Lord Bayley (Fig 26). That was in 1811, therefore it is unlikely that the regiment, although on the British side, could have worn the blue uniform which became regulation in the following year. This closely resembled the British light infantry pattern, except that the facings were red for all units, the only, rather inadequate distinction being the initial letter of the regiment's name on the collar, since spanish regiments were not numbered.

The foregoing emphasises still further the complex politics of Spain. It will be recalled that after Trafalgar in 1805, Napoleon, apprehensive of a British attack via Portugal and Spain, required the former country to close her ports to Great Britain, and Charles of Spain to allow French troops to cross his country. The King agreed, and by the secret Treaty of Fontainebleau of October 7, 1807, committed himself to support the French with Spanish troops. Accordingly, a French corps of 30,000 men under Junot was sent to Lisbon. The Prince Regent of Portugal fled the country, and the whole of Portugal was occupied by the French.

Next, a force of 15,000 Spaniards under the Marquis de la Romana was sent to assist the French in the Baltic area, and French troops numbering some 100,000 men occupied Spain.

All this was rather too much for the Spanish people. They forced King Charles to abdicate in favour of his son Ferdinand; but Napoleon refused to recognise the new king and persuaded the Council of Regency to give the throne to his brother Joseph, then King of Naples.

For the Spaniards, this was the last straw. Both Spain and Portugal rose against the French, and from 1818 onwards no Frenchman was safe from the terrible practices of the *guerrilleros*.

SPANISH INFANTRY 1812
Battalion Companies (marching order)
SHAKO: White tuft and bands; red cockade; brass lion.
JACKET: Blue; red collar, cuffs, turnbacks, piping; brass buttons.
TROUSERS, GAITERS: Blue-grey.
EQUIPMENT: Grey roll; brown pack and water-bottle; white belts, straps, haversack.
(after Conde de Clonard: "Hist. . . d. Ejer. Esp.")

SPANISH INFANTRY 1812
Light Companies
SHAKO: Green tuft and bands; red cockade; brass bugle.
JACKET: Blue; red collar, cuffs, turnbacks, piping; brass buttons; green fringe under blue wing; white belts.
TROUSERS, GAITERS: Blue-grey.
(after Conde de Clonard: "Hist. . . d. Ejer. Esp.")

FRENCH NATIONAL GUARD

It comes as something of a surprise to find that units of the National Guard appear in the French orders of battle. These troops, in function somewhat reminiscent of the British Territorial Army, were not intended to serve outside the frontiers of the French Empire, but since the frontiers were continually shifting it was probably not difficult for the Authorities to apply a very elastic scale. For instance, many cohorts were sent to Germany after the Campaign in Russia.

The National Guard was organised in cohorts, which were the equivalent of battalions in the regular army; and several cohorts formed one legion. Thus we find that the *Légion de Midi* was mobilised in 1809 : a unit which had probably nothing to do with the earlier legion of that name, raised on April 27, 1792, and dressed in light blue.

All the legions were clothed alike in dark blue jackets with red collars and cuffs, and regulation shakos—in other words, the standard infantry uniform—but with silver buttons and attributes and epaulettes of the same for the officers (a pattern incidentally, later adopted by the British Militia).

The legions of the *Landes* and of the *Basses-Pyrénées* were present at the battle of the Pyrenees, and were doubtless dressed as the others.

On May 13, 1812 the National Guard was organised on a basis of three distinct age-groups. The first was for the men of 20 to 26 years of age who belonged to the 1st six conscript classes, but who had not been called up because their units were complete. The second included men aged 27 to 40, and the third was for those of 41 to 60.

PAGE 66: This famous Caton Woodville print of 1894 depicts the Duke of Wellington surveying the scene after the taking of Badajos in April 1812. This walled town was breached and taken by men of the 4th and Light Divisions in one of the bloodiest actions of the campaign. Over 3,500 British troops were killed or wounded in the assault. Men of the various regiments in the divisions are portrayed on the right. On the left are the remains of the chevaux de frise which formed a major obstacle to the attacking infantry (A. H. Bowling collection).

ABOVE: A Harry Payne print depicting a British line infantry regiment at Albuhera in 1811. The facings are buff and the drummer (foreground) has the reversed colours on his tunic, ie, scarlet facings on a buff coat. His belt plate identifies the regiment as the 31st Foot, though they in fact, wore single loops not doubles. Note the colour sergeant with pike covering the ensign with the colour (A. H. Bowling collection).

Appendix 1: Chronology of Main Events and Battles

1808 Hostilities commenced August 1808. British under General Wellesley (later Duke of Wellington) land in Portugal (at Mondego Bay).

Aug 17: British defeat French under General Laborde at Rolica.

Aug 21: Battle of Vimiera; Wellesley defeats Junot. French agree (Convention of Cintra) to evacuate Portugal.

Sept 30: French evacuation of Portugal completed.

Nov 30: Spaniards defeated at Tudela. British Army under Sir John Moore advances from Portugal into Spain.

Dec 22: British Army joins a force under Baird from Corunna, but not being properly supported by the Spaniards, and being threatened by superior force under Napoleon and Soult, Moore retires on Corunna.

1809

Jan 16: Battle of Corunna, British beat off French and secure re-embarkation of the army (for Lisbon).

Feb 21: Saragossa taken by French.

April 22: Wellesley again in command at Lisbon.

May 12: Passage of the Douro. Wellesley enters Spain with mixed British and Spanish force.

July 27-28: Wellesley defeats French at Talavera. Not receiving reinforcements he retires on Almeida.

Nov 20: Spanish defeat at Ocana; French overrun South of Spain. In the winter Wellington forms the fortified lines of Torres Vedras to cover Lisbon. and provide a secure base resting on the sea for his army.

1810

July: French under Massena again invade Portugal.

July 11: They take Cuidad Rodrigo.

Sept 27: Battle of Busaco; Wellington defeats the French. After the battle he retires slowly on lines of Torres Vedras.

Nov 14: Massena, unable to attack the lines, or to maintain himself longer in front of them for want of supplies, begins to retreat towards Spanish frontier.

1811

Feb 19: Battle of Gebora; Soult defeats Spaniards and then takes Badajos.

March 5: Battle of Barossa; Graham defeats Victor; Wellington having been reinforced follows Massena.

April 3: Battle of Sabugal: Massena is defeated and retires from Portugal; Wellington besieges Almeida.

May 5: Battle of Fuentes de Oñoro; Massena advancing to the relief of Almeida is again defeated by, Wellington; Almeida surrenders. Wellington then besieges Badajos but fails to reduce it.

May 16: Soult marching to relief of Badajos is defeated at Battle of Albuhera.

Sept 10: Battle of Ximena; Spaniards defeat French.

Oct 28: Battle of Merida; Hill defeats French.

(continued overleaf)

1812

Jan 4: Battle of Lake Albufera; Suchet defeats Spaniards.

Jan 19: Wellington takes Cuidad Rodrigo by storm.

April 6: He takes Badajos by storm and then advances into Spain.

April 6: Defeat of Soult of Llerena.

July 12: Battle of Salamanca; Wellington defeats French under Mormont.

Aug 12: Wellington enters Madrid. Unable to maintain himself here through Spaniards failing to guard his communications, he retires to borders of Portugal.

1813

April 13: Battle of Castalla; Murray defeats Suchet.

June 21: Battle of Vittoria; Wellington defeats King Joseph.

July 28 until Aug 2: Battles of the Pyrenees; Wellington defeats Soult.

Aug 31: St. Sebastian stormed by Graham.

Nov 10: Wellington defeats Soult at Nivelle and enters France.

Dec 9 to 13: Passage of the Nive by Wellington.

1814

Feb 27: Wellington defeats Soult at Orthes

Mar 30: Wellington defeats Soult at Tarbes.

April 10: Battle of Toulouse; final defeat of Soult by Wellington.

May 30: Peace of Paris; Napoleon, having abdicated, is given the island of Elba. Bourbons restored in France.

Appendix 2: Books for further reading

The following books include accounts of the battles of the Peninsular War and coverage of the campaign generally:

Battlefields of Europe, Vol 1, edited by D. Chandler (Hugh Evelyn)

History of the British Army, Young and Lawford.

Encyclopaedia of Military History, Dupuy and Dupuy (Macdonald).

Dictionary of Battles (Rupert Hart-Davis).

A History of the Regiments and Uniforms of the British Army, Barnes (Seeley Service).

History of the Peninsular War, Charles Oman